LOVE MY RIFLE
MORE THAN YOU

LOVE MY RIFLE
MORE THAN YOU

Young and Female in the US Army

Kayla Williams

with Michael E. Staub

Weidenfeld & Nicolson
LONDON

First published in the USA in 2005
by W.W. Norton & Company
First published in Great Britain in 2006
by Weidenfeld & Nicolson

1 3 5 7 9 10 8 6 4 2

This is a work of non-fiction, and the events it recounts are true.
However, the names and certain identifying characteristics of
some of the people who appear in its pages have been changed.
The views expressed in this book are the author's and do not
necessarily represent the views of the Department of Defense
or its components.

Thanks to Captain Brian Johns for permission to reprint
his contributions to the chapter, How to Prepare for
Deployment to Iraq.

A CIP catalogue record for this book
is available from the British Library

ISBN-10 0 297 84874 7
ISBN-13 9 780 297 84874 5

Printed in Great Britain by Clays Ltd, St Ives plc

Weidenfeld & Nicolson
An imprint of the Orion Publishing Group
Orion House, 5 Upper St Martin's Lane,
London WC2H 9EA

www.orionbooks.co.uk

For Brian—
Who gives me hope.

Cindy, Cindy, Cindy Lou
Love my rifle more than you
You used to be my beauty queen
Now I love my M-16.

—ARMY MARCHING CADENCE

CONTENTS

PROLOGUE

SOMETIMES, EVEN NOW, I wake up before dawn and forget I am not a slut. The air is not quite dark, not quite light, and I lie absolutely still, trying to will myself to remember that that is *not* what I am. Sometimes, on better mornings, it comes to me right away. And then there are all those other times.

Slut.

The only other choice is bitch. If you're a woman and a soldier, those are the choices you get.

I'm twenty-eight years old. Military Intelligence, five years, here and in Iraq. One of the 15 percent of the U.S. military that's female. And that whole 15 percent trying to get past an old joke. "What's the difference between a bitch and slut? A slut will fuck anyone, a bitch will fuck anyone but you." So if she's nice or friendly, outgoing or chatty—she's a slut. If she's distant or reserved or professional—she's a bitch.

A woman soldier has to toughen herself up. Not just for the enemy, for battle, or for death. I mean toughen herself to spend months awash in a sea of nervy, hyped-up guys who, when they're not thinking about getting killed, are thinking about getting laid. Their eyes on you all the time, your breasts, your ass—like there is nothing else to watch, no sun, no river, no desert, no mortars at night.

Still, it's more complicated than that. Because at the same time you soften yourself up. Their eyes, their hunger: yes, it's shaming—but they also make you special. I don't like to say it—it cuts you inside—but the attention, the admiration, the *need*: they make you powerful. If you're a woman in the Army, it doesn't matter so much about your looks. What counts is that you are female.

Wartime makes it worse. There's the killing on the streets, the bombs at the checkpoints—and the combat in the tents. Some women sleep around: lots of sex with lots of guys, in sleeping bags, in trucks, in sand, in America, in Iraq. Some women hold themselves back; they avoid sex like it's some weapon of mass destruction. I know about both.

And I know about something else. How these same guys you want to piss on become *your* guys. Another girl enters your tent, and they look at her the way they looked at you, and what drove you crazy with anger suddenly drives you crazy with jealousy. They're *yours*. Fuck, you left your husband to be with them, you walked out on him for them. These guys, they're your husband, they're your father, your brother, your lover—your life.

I never thought I would feel this way—not about these guys, not about this war, not even about my country. I was a punk-kid rebel, and now I'm part of the most authoritarian institution imaginable. I thought this war was probably wrong, didn't want to go. The lies that got us there, that killed some of us, that wounded and maimed more of us: Only the most messed-up-patriotic-head-up-his-ass-blind-faith-my-country-right-or-wrong soldier believed them.

But now I watch a cheesy commercial for Anheuser-Busch of

civilians applauding troops returning from Iraq and I get all emotional. I also watch videos on the Internet, with combat footage—"Let the Bodies Hit the Floor" and "Red, White, and Blue (The Angry American)"—and it chokes me up. It's scary to think about how much being in the Army has changed me. That experience couldn't leave even the strongest person the same. Everything I thought I knew about what it would be like turned out to be wrong. Not reality.

So I wanted to write a book to let people know what it *feels* like to be a woman soldier in peace and in war. I wanted to capture the terror, the mind-numbing tedium; and the joy and the honor. Not overlooking the suicidal periods, the anorexic impulses, the promiscuity; and the comradeship and the bravery. The times we were scared out of our minds. The times we were bored out of our minds, too. No one has ever written that book— about what life is like for the 15 percent. Don't count Jessica Lynch. Her story meant nothing to us. The same goes for Lynndie England. I'm not either of them, and neither are any of the real women I know in the service.

In a dress, away from the base, you'd never guess I was a soldier. Always been a girl that catches a guy's eyes. And yet I do fifty-five push-ups in under a minute. Tough, and proud to be tough. I love my M-4, the smell of it, of cleaning fluid, of gunpowder: the smell of strength. Gun in your hands, and you're in a special place. I've come to look forward to that.

It can turn you, though. Women are no different from men in their corruptibility. Women are just as competent—and just as incompetent.

As I write this in the early months of 2005, 91 percent of all Army career fields are now open to women, and 67 percent of

Army positions can be filled by women. Women are currently authorized to sign up for 87 percent of all enlisted military occupational specialties (MOS). But isn't Congress keeping women out of combat? There are no women in artillery, no women in the infantry. We are not permitted to drive tanks. We can't be Rangers or Special Forces. There are also some teams we rarely go out with because the gear is considered too heavy for the average female to hump on her back.

So people conclude that girls don't do combat zones. That we're somewhere else from where the action is. But that's bullshit. We are Marines. We are Military Police. We are there as support to the infantry in almost every way you might imagine. We even act in support roles for the Special Forces. We carry weapons—and we use them. We may kick down doors when an Iraqi village gets cleared. We do crowd control. We are also often the soldiers who negotiate with the locals—nearly one third of Military Intelligence (MI), where I work, is female.

Insurgents' mortar attacks reach us, too. In fact, because insurgents strike supply routes so often, it's frequently the non-infantry soldiers like us—with fewer up-armored vehicles—who end up getting hit and engaging in combat.

In Iraq, I cleaned blood from soldiers' gear after a roadside bomb hit a convoy. I saw the bloodied bodies of locals—civilians caught in the wrong place at the wrong time. I saw death. I speak Arabic, so I participated in interrogations. I had to deal with the tension between wanting to help the locals and having to do battle with them. I pointed my weapon at a child. I've understood things and seen things I need to forget: Humiliation. Torture. It was not just Abu Ghraib—it happened elsewhere, too.

Sometimes I wake up and I feel frightened all over again. The darkness is like the blackest night on the mountains west of Mosul, no moon, no stars, no light anywhere in the whole freaking world. I want so very much to vanish from the planet. Just evaporate like vapor trails after the jets have gone.

The smell of dead animals being burned. Dogs barking as I pull guard in the night. The different soils. The day we found dead white chickens everywhere and thought it was due to a chemical attack. How the faces of local women, and especially little girls, just *lit up* with pleasure at the sight of a female soldier: shy smiles. Saddam's palaces—marble, multiple colors, cut into designs and layered, incredibly beautiful and obscenely expensive.

I don't forget. I can't forget any of it. From basic training all the way to Iraq and back home again.

QUEEN FOR A YEAR

Queen for a Year: **1 a:** any American female stationed overseas in a predominantly male military environment. **b:** a female soldier who becomes stuck-up during her deployment due to an exponential increase in male attention—used disparagingly.

RIGHT INTO IT: Sex is key to any woman soldier's experiences in the American military. No one likes to acknowledge it, but there's a strange sexual allure to being a woman and a soldier.

I mean sex while in Iraq. At war. While deployed.

Take this one girl. I heard from reliable sources in Iraq she gave head to every guy in her unit. I mean, I heard it from guys who were there. Participants. No rumor. Truth. Guys who'd meet me and say: *Hey, Kayla, I'm told* all *MI females really like to* . . .

Don't get me wrong. I've never much minded the taste of it myself. I just had to wonder: Where was the pleasure in this for *her*? Was she nuts? And meanwhile, she's making my life tons more difficult. Making it tougher for the rest of us females to get our work done without having guys insinuate that *blow jobs* was part of our Advanced Individual Training. It totally sucked, pun intended. It made it easy for guys over there to treat females as if we were less reliable. Which is enraging, since our skills as *soldiers* are what landed us in this war in the first place. Anyway, this particular girl got caught in the act, I guess you could say. More than once. Reprimanded for dereliction of duty. Almost comical when you really stop to think about it.

Or the twenty girls from this one unit who got sent home from Iraq pregnant. Knocked up. I heard a number of married guys were involved in this situation. Now that's a violation of the Uniform Code of Military Justice. Single girls and single guys can do as they please. Technically.

A woman at war: you're automatically a desirable commodity, and a scarce one at that. We call it "Queen for a Year." Even the unattractive girls start to act stuck-up. It's impossible not to notice.

"Queen for a Year." You won't find the phrase in the dictionary or any compilation of military terms. But say it among soldiers, and they'll know immediately what you mean. That's what we've called American women at war since nurses traveled to Vietnam in the sixties.

There's also this "deployment scale" for hotness. Let me explain. On a scale of ten, say she's a five. You know—average looks, maybe a little mousy, nothing special. But okay. Not a girl who gets second glances in civilian life. But in the Army, while we're deployed? Easily an eight. One hot babe. On average *every* girl probably gets three extra points on a ten-point scale. Useful. After you're in-country for a few months, all the girls begin to look good—or at least *better*. It changes—how should I say this?—

the *dynamics* of being deployed.

You could get things easier, and you could get out of things easier. For a girl there were lots of little things you could do to make your load while deployed a whole lot lighter. You could use your femaleness to great advantage. You could do less work, get more assistance, and receive more special favors. Getting supplies? Working on the trucks? It could be a cinch—if you wanted it to be. It didn't take much. A little went a long way. Some of us worked it to the bone. Who says the life of the Army girl has to be cruel?

Lots of girls succumbed to temptation. The younger girls were the most susceptible. Many thrived and fed on the male attention they were getting for the first time in their lives.

I did my personal best to resist. So did my friends and the girls I respected. (That's why I respected them.) But many girls became full-fledged Queens for a Year. We saw it. And the guys talked.

The guys loved to talk. It didn't even especially matter what girls did or did not do. By the time it circled back to us (and in Iraq, everything that went around came around extra-fast), it might as well have been true.

"I watched her doing PT today. She was doing dips. She wants it!"

"I saw her in line for chow—she was wearing a tight brown T-shirt. She's looking for some action!"

Creepy.

And the locals? Even worse than Joes. At least some American guys have learned some subtlety about staring at our tits. They'd look out of the corner of their eyes. Or when we were looking away. Either Iraqi guys didn't care or didn't have the practice.

They just blatantly and openly stared at our tits. *All the time.*

Apparently Iraqis asked our guys if we were prostitutes. Employed by the U.S. military to service the troops in the same way the Russian army managed sex for its soldiers in Kosovo. I didn't want *anyone* to think we were the U.S. equivalent of that!

None of this means that life in the Army while deployed to a combat zone has to be celibate. "What goes TDY stays TDY." It's a longstanding military tradition. License to do as we please while on "temporary duty"—that is, while away from our permanent post. And it stays TDY when we return home.

Sex is not specifically prohibited for deployed soldiers. It's just *implied* that it is not allowed. Yet the PX in Iraq sells condoms. The general attitude is: "Don't get caught." The one rule is: "Be discreet." Probably most of the single girls do it. Most of the single guys, too, if they ever get the chance. It becomes a simple matter of supply and demand.

And even though it's not okay, it's true—if a girl was indiscreet, if she got caught, or people knew, everyone lost respect for her. Like she was some slut. It was different, of course, for the guys. Somehow everyone got it that getting laid was okay for the guys.

So get real. The Army is not a monastery. More like a fraternity. Or a massive frat party. With weapons. With girls there for the taking—at least some of the time.

The guys are there for the taking too. And we took. I took.

But mostly I chose to be a bitch. I was nowhere as young as most of the other girls over there. Nowhere as innocent—at all. I'd hung around guys almost all my life; my punk rock scene in high school was overwhelmingly male. I'd dealt with sex from a young age. I'd been married.

In Iraq I felt I could deal with being Queen for a Year. But it still got to me. It still got me angry. Sometimes. I remember walking through the chow hall (once it was built) at the airfield was like running a gauntlet of eyes. Guys stared and stared and stared. Sometimes it felt like I was some fucking zoo animal. Guys hitting on us or saying inappropriate things—just *constant*.

Then sometimes I got in the mood. I'd enter the chow hall with a swing to my step. Check me out. Look. Don't touch. So occasionally it went to my head.

The girls joked, too. Some guys we met in Iraq were no prime specimens themselves. Funny nose, bad posture, bad teeth, whatever. But they also looked better. Always. So it worked both ways. Location, location, location. It played with all our minds.

It was like a separate bloodless war within the larger deadly one.

Let me tell you a story.

"Hey, Kayla! Show us your boobs!"

I was on a mountain near the Syrian border. At this time, I may well have been the most forward-deployed female soldier in Iraq. You could lose yourself in the view from up there, especially at dusk or dawn, when the sheer impact of the vista made your head spin.

I was alone. Alone with the guys, that is. For weeks.

They're frustrated. Horny. Talking openly about jerking off.

We sat in the blazing sun—*hot*—not doing much.

"Show us your tits, bitch!" Trash talk.

"No."

"C'mon, Kayla. Lift your T-shirt. For a second. Please! Let us see what you've got!"

"No."

I had no *principled* objection. I'd modeled nude for art classes in college. I had no qualms about showing my body.

Then the guys made what I considered their first real mistake. They started to ante up. Ten bucks. Twenty. Forty. Sixty-five. Eighty bucks. It went to eighty-seven dollars, and then a smart-ass threw in some M&M's he'd stashed.

They came to me with their proposition.

"C'mon, Kayla. This is hard-earned American money. Uncle Sam's almighty dollar. Plus M&M's. We know how much you like M&M's. Now show us your damn tits!"

"Fuck off, assholes!"

It was over. Because I might *remotely* have done it for free. I would *never* do it for money. What did these guys think I was? A whore?

WHO I WAS

Hot.

As a small child, I reached up to touch the stove. To play with fire. Then pulled back in a flash. And spoke my first word.

"Hot."

I always liked this detail about myself. That I neither cried in pain nor called for *mama* or *dada*. I always thought it said something about me, though I've been torn about what it said. That I was willing to venture out and take the risk, and report clearly on what I had learned? That's the perspective I prefer and like to think is true. But on darker days (and there have been plenty of those), I think this early encounter with fire left me deeply hesitant to take risks for fear of pain. As a consequence I've always believed that I have something to prove.

Especially to myself.

It's a terrible thing to think that fear of pain or of failure shadows your entire existence. It's a worse thing to believe that you must struggle against those fears *every day of your life*. To prove to yourself and the world that you can do it. You can take risks. You are not afraid and will never be afraid.

I can admit it. I've been afraid. I've always been afraid. But

I'm most afraid I'll pass up a chance to overcome my fears.

Hence the Army? Not so fast. Nothing is as simple as that. We'll get there when we get there.

Growing up, my favorite drug was LSD. If you think about it, this makes sense. Marijuana made me groggy and slow-witted. I could never concentrate when I was high. Everything moved in absurd slow motion. People giggled like idiots and acted all profound while making no sense at all. I hated the experience. Who wanted to sound stupid? Not me. So I dropped acid, and it delivered a crystallized sense of lucidity in which my brain spun so quickly and lurched here and there in ways I could barely keep up with. But I did keep up. I always kept up. I don't recall having the notorious bad trip, only the lukewarm trip—the one that left me unenlightened (but hardly undeterred). But acid always made me think. And I loved (and love) to think.

Life in a combat zone made me think, too. Deployment in Iraq was like this yearlong invitation to think, though a year was probably way too much time. There was the war, but the war (as reported at the time) ended in May 2003. We'd only been in-country for a couple of months. Then came supposed peace. And during the peace, at least until the war began again, there was more time to sit around between missions. You started to go crazy with the thinking and the waiting and the sitting around. And the bullshit. You wondered what life might be like without so much time to think. You thought about how much you were thinking. You thought about thinking about thinking. Like an acid trip without the acid or the trip. Just thoughts. What fun was that?

I can't explain my attitude toward risk taking. Is it contradictory? There are things I've done, and there are things I'd never do. For instance I've gone to bars and drunk since I was thirteen. But I refused to get my first tattoo until I was eighteen, when it was legal to do so. (I now have six.) I would not get in a car with a drunk driver. I would never take that risk. But I've had lots of unprotected sex over the years. And I've let homeless guys I've never met before stay over in my house. Those risks I would take.

But before I get too far, let me say a few words about Mom and Dad.

My mom was a Republican with an antiauthoritarian streak, and my dad was a former pot smoker with anger-management problems. Mom had been married twice before; her first ex-husband had custody of her kids, and she didn't see them much. Dad had been divorced once; his ex-wife was a hippie who had lived on a commune in Washington State. Many years later, long after my folks split up, we all went out to Washington to attend the wedding of his daughter from his first marriage. We stayed with his ex-wife. Everyone got along fine. My mother, my stepmother, and my dad's first ex-wife liked to joke "There are three Mrs. Williams in the room."

Dad's daughter, my half-sister, Yarrow, was the sane one in my family. Kind and loving and generous, she was twelve years older than me. Mom said that when she'd first met Yarrow, she'd immediately thought about my dad: "This guy's got good genes." And decided she wanted his child. Years later Dad told me he'd felt used by Mom—tricked by her—and that he had not wanted another child then. I didn't really want to hear it. But at that point he wanted to come clean and build a better relationship with me.

My parents married, and I was born a couple of years later.

And a year or so after that, Mom bundled me into her car and left my dad. Said she wanted to raise this child alone, maybe as recompense for losing her other children to her first husband. Who knows?

Anyway, so ended the story of Mom and Dad. I certainly continued to see Dad throughout my childhood, and he certainly continued to have his tantrums. When I was still small, he grabbed me by my ponytail and threw me onto my bed so hard I smacked my head. Or the time I got muddy once while we were camping, and he ordered me to strip. So I lay huddled, freezing and naked, in the backseat of our car while he washed my clothes at a Laundromat—all the time berating me for ruining our vacation. I must have been five or six. Though he could be kind sometimes, too. I remember he made me this excellent robot costume for Halloween once, and he made cool snow dragons (instead of snowmen) and sprayed them with green food dye and gave them red tongues. He was always *trying* to be a good dad, even though it was obvious it didn't come naturally to him.

Mom was an artist from a well-to-do family, but she seemed intent on having us slide down the social ladder as much as possible. Her life played like Horatio Alger in reverse: riches to rags. Maybe it wasn't her fault, I don't know. At first things were good, though the neighborhood in Columbus, Ohio, she found for us after she left Dad was so sketchy some of my friends from school were never permitted to visit. But Mom got me into an outstanding private school with all these wealthy kids. So I moved between these two worlds—privileged and poor.

The school was multicultural and had a terrific curriculum. I started French lessons when I was really young, and Mom was so pleased that she somehow managed to take me to France twice so I could improve my language skills. Awesome experiences. So she clearly cared that I become intellectual, and put energy into that. I enjoyed being around all these bright kids during the day, and I did well in school. Meanwhile our finances remained okay for a while. She had solid connections in the gallery and crafts-show scene, and her sculptures and carvings sold.

Everything changed when I was nine or so. A serious financial setback coincided with health problems for my mother, and things got very rough. I remember peering around the door-frame, watching her going through the bills, trying to make her money stretch. Crying that we were three months behind on rent.

Things never got good again after that. We never regained our footing. There was not much money for toys, movies, vacations, treats; no money for new clothes for me at the start of a new school year. Little money for food, even, and eventually we had to collect food stamps so we could eat. Mom—a Republican, remember?—hated that we were living on public assistance. She hated people on public assistance, and now here she was, one of those people. She thought people on public assistance should wear orange jumpsuits and live in workhouses. Still does.

My mom—coming from Oklahoma country—felt it was an obligation for any child of hers to learn how to shoot a gun. Essential life skill, that's all. So when I was ten years old, the time came for me to learn. She drove me down to some weirdo's private land, and the people there handed me a .22. The thing felt *heavy*. Then they gave me a .38, and finally a rifle—but that was too much for me to lift. I never forgot how to handle a weapon. More than a dozen years later, at boot camp, these memories came right back again like déjà vu.

Age twelve: I switched to public school for high school to save money. Suddenly I was this brainy geek, feeling rejected because I was smart. So I rejected everyone instead. And became a punk. A lot of punks I met were the same way.

I got into the punk and alternative scene when I was thirteen. I loved the music. (Still do.) Jane's Addiction. Violent Femmes. Fugazi. The Dead Kennedys. I began to hang around seventeen- and eighteen-year-old high-school dropouts. Everyone so fucking *angry* all the time. Ronald Reagan had fueled our collective rage at societal injustice. We got pissed off about racism and classism, but mostly it was about the music. We saw all the shows. I attended the first Lollapalooza back in 1991. And since the punk movement in Columbus was so small, it overlapped with every other marginal scene—Goth, Skater, even neo-Nazi—and we all ended up together at the same shows. So things blurred.

I wore the combat boots. I looked tough. Intimidating. People locked their car doors when I walked by. That was cool. But it also infuriated me. I believed this was prejudice. I developed a sense of kinship with black people. People judged me on my appearance—just like white racism. I didn't think: Lose the look and I'd be just a good lily-white girl again. I thought: Fuck America! I was thirteen. There were a lot of things I didn't fully understand.

I did understand that the punk scene got me out of the house. Gave me a community. Like a family. And got me into a few tight situations. Like when I ran away from home for a few weeks the summer I was thirteen.

That was a risk that made sense to me.

As a runaway, I hung with Allison. Allison was fifteen with a

Mohawk and braces. Allison was convinced that Missing Persons had photographs of her, and so Allison decided to alter her appearance. I remember the night I watched her untwist her braces—she pried them off with scissors. She was so proud of herself when she got them off. And I looked at her and I laughed. Here's this fifteen-year-old girl with a fucking Mohawk who somehow thought that undoing her braces was going to help her escape notice.

We got ourselves into a bad situation toward the end. We stayed at a house we called the Dog Shit House because there were pit bulls everywhere and no one picked up the shit. The place was disgusting. We crashed there until I found a box of literature and began to look through it. It was neo-Nazi propaganda, and I was still a little too naive to be sure what I was reading. I remember here I was with Allison—a Jewish girl—in this neo-Nazi filth palace. Then one of the neo-Nazis found a picture in my bag of an African American friend from my school. "Who the fuck is this?" Then all the guys began to flip out on Allison and me. "Who the fuck is this nigger?" One of them grabbed my bag and set it on fire, while another one got a gun. But no bullets. Ended up throwing the gun at me while they chased me down the street. (Allison stayed at the Dog Shit House, but she had to fuck a guy to do it.) I ran to a house and begged the people to let me in. "I'm being chased by neo-Nazis!" I slept on their couch and returned home the next day. But my mother had changed the locks on me.

A couple of years after that, my mom ended up throwing me out of the house. She'd found evidence I was using drugs and wanted me out immediately.

That's when I moved to Kentucky to live with my father. But

I was already thinking: If this didn't work out, if my father threw me out of *his* house, I'd be homeless. And *that* was not a risk I was willing to take. I knew I couldn't handle a JDC (juvenile detention center). The very thought freaked me out. Scared me straight, I guess you could say. So I graduated from high school at sixteen and went directly to college.

But I couldn't see any point to it. I felt overwhelmed, so I dropped out of college after freshman year. Moved back to Columbus, and heroin had hit the streets. Everyone had just seen the film *Trainspotting* and deemed it exceptionally cool. Shooting heroin was suddenly very cool. A lot of my punk rock friends and acquaintances were using, and here I was trying to hold down a job as a secretary. I was hanging around homeless punks at night and on weekends, many of whom were doing hard drugs, and I was going to an office during the week.

I had vowed I would always support myself. And here were my friends calling me a poser because I worked in an office and dressed in nice clothes. I didn't know what to say besides, "Fuck off! You're eating my food. At least someone here has a job." Around this time, too, I noticed the sexism of the punk rock scene. I'd taken a couple of women's studies courses that made me think more about issues like feminism and misogyny. And here were these punk rockers treating me like a girl, and I hated it.

"How you gonna dis your bros for just some girl?" they'd say to one another. So that's all I was to them. *Just some girl.* That's all I'd ever been to them. It really pissed me off. That and the fact I was hanging around a guy, Douglas, who was knocking me around, persuaded me to finish college after all. Get out of Columbus. Get a degree. Not end up a loser like these losers.

I graduated from Bowling Green State University when I was

twenty. I graduated cum laude with my entering class even though I had missed a year. By the time I was twenty-two, I was employed in Tampa, Florida, by Infinite OutSource, a fundraising collective funded by the Corporation for Public Broadcasting. I was raising more than five million dollars a year through direct mail and telemarketing for fifteen television and radio stations nationwide. I owned my first house, and I earned a salary of thirty thousand dollars a year. I was getting job offers in the nonprofit world for twice as much money. But I was also wanting to make a change.

I was feeling as if I had never really challenged myself. I felt I'd never learned how to fail. I'd never lost my fear of failure. I was at a point in my life when I felt that if I didn't do something drastic, I was going to wake up in a house with a white picket fence and a minivan and kids who hated me.

My love life? Complicated as always.

Before I got my house, I had rented a room in my apartment to a girl who worked as a stripper. She started to date a Saudi. Tariq was a friend of the Saudi guy. That's how he and I first met.

It's funny. Meeting a Muslim through a stripper strikes me as funny.

Tariq—everyone called him Rick—came over and we'd talk. We went on a first date. (He forgot his wallet and insisted I wait at the restaurant while he drove home to get it so he could pay for dinner.)

Rick observed Ramadan—kind of. He wouldn't drink alcohol or smoke cigarettes during the day. But he worked in a liquor store. He would not have sex if the Koran was in the room with us. So we moved it out.

Rick was Muslim in the way that most Christians are

Christian. Christians believe all kinds of things. "I believe pre-marital sex is wrong." But they don't follow their beliefs. "Yeah, I *believe* it's wrong—but I'm still going to do it."

We never lived together. But eventually he began to stay at my house every single night. We also shared a car for a while, when his car broke down. But he always kept his own apartment. I'd suggest: "We could pool our resources." But it was important to him to maintain his own space.

Rick's rich Kuwaiti and Saudi friends had everything. Ahmed's father bought him a Porsche. The other Ahmed's father bought him a house to live in for a year even before he started college so he could practice his English. Their families bought them everything. But aside from coming to America to get a fantastic education, these guys were also in the States to sleep with American women. To get it out of their system, so they could go home and marry good Muslim girls. They even admitted it. "Yes. That's exactly what happens." They couldn't fuck around with good Muslim girls back home. So they came to the States. They went to college. They slept with American girls. Then they went home and settled down.

They didn't think twice about it. Same with most Arabic women. They boarded a plane for the States and changed out of their *hijabs* in the cramped lavatories—and put on make-up, Chanel dresses, and high heels.

Rick was nothing like his friends. Rick worked two jobs so he could afford community college. I respected him for trying to make his own way in the world.

Rick was gifted at languages. He spoke Arabic, Greek, English, French, and Russian. Born in Jordan, he spent the first five years of his life in Lebanon. His mother told me stories of

Beirut during the civil war. She described how her five- and seven-year-old children buried their faces in her lap and wept while bombs fell around them. She said she prayed simply for her family to survive each day. I could not imagine what this would be like for a mother.

She made me think about how we—as Americans—are so willing to bomb other people's countries.

Rick and I were together for two years. He taught me words in his dialect in Arabic. I shopped for vegetarian products in the neighborhood Middle Eastern stores. I learned to love the cadences of the language. All the people in the shops were so encouraging and helpful. Was I married to a Muslim? Or was I Lebanese myself? Apparently my eyes and skin tone allowed me to pass for Lebanese, which surprised me. "No. I'm not Lebanese." But they remained just as friendly and kind. Just as eager to help me improve my few Arabic words.

I saw an intimacy to the Arab community in Tampa that I envied. Everyone was so close in a way I never experienced in white America—certainly not at college or growing up in Columbus. You need a new carburetor for your car? Take it to a friend's garage and get it replaced extra cheap. You need money? Friends lend it to you. The community was like a family, and people respected and trusted one another more than I'd ever experienced. Maybe in small towns it's like this, or certainly in some other ethnic communities you still see it. And when my older sister, Yarrow, was dying of cancer, I saw how members of her church brought food to her husband and made sure he was doing okay. But in big cities or many other places in America? Forget it.

It wasn't until I joined the military that I experienced anything like this again. In the military you'd be moving into your barracks, and you'd be having trouble hauling your shit, and someone would immediately drop everything to help you. They don't know who you are. They don't give a fuck who you are, but you're wearing the same uniform and they immediately help you. That's the way it works in the military.

I came to love Rick's willingness to share his community with me. I was honored to be a part of it for the two years we were together. It was tough, really tough, to let go.

As our relationship became more serious, we began to look at each other a little differently. I started to ask myself: Could I marry this person? If we're going to have a committed future together, how do things need to be between us?

I criticized Rick, but if anyone else criticized him or how he treated me, I got defensive. We'd been dating for six months when he picked me up from work. My coworkers knew I was dating a Muslim. And I thought they knew me. The very next day a woman from work said to me: "Oh, he doesn't look like anything I expected." At the time Rick had a ponytail and an earring. I snapped at her: "What did you expect? A turban and a camel?" Whether she could admit it or not, that was absolutely what she expected. She thought: Muslim. One word. And instantly she had a picture in her head.

My mom told me: "You shouldn't marry Rick because your aunt's husband is Muslim—and that's been so hard for her." I said: "They're still married after thirty years! They're happy and love each other. You've been divorced three times. Do you think I am really going to listen to marriage advice from you?!"

At the same time Rick said that if he had kids he didn't know if he'd want to raise them in America. I understood what he meant. If I had a daughter, I don't know if I would want to raise her in the circumstances I'd known as a girl. Once Rick and I were in Sears waiting for my alternator to get fixed. A man and a woman and their kid came into the garage office. The girl was about ten years old. Way prepubescent. She wore low-slung tight hip-hugger jeans, a pink skin-tight tank top with little straps, and little strappy sandals. She swayed her hips when she walked. Rick shook his head. Disgusted by the extent to which we sexualize children in our society—and the extent to which we allow children to sexualize themselves.

On other occasions Rick said to me: "You know, you shouldn't wear that tank top. If you wear that tank top, people will judge you in a certain way. They are not going to listen to what you have to say. And you're smart. I want people to judge you for what you have to say—not just for how you look."

Rick acted more like a traditional—or stereotypical—Muslim the longer we were together.

When I was just an American chick he slept with—or whatever—it was no big deal for him. What did he care what I acted like? But as things got more serious and I started to look more like wife material than fucking material, he wanted to control me more.

He'd say: *You can't behave like this. . . . You can't do this. . . . You can't wear that.*

Don't get me wrong: I've dated Catholic guys who were far worse.

When a personality conflict with a new female superior got me fired from my job in October 1999, I fell into a bad depression. Rick took care of me. He brought me flowers and orange

juice. He mowed my lawn and made sure I was okay. I appreciated how *genuine* he was—how it was never just words with him.
He never gave me a line about how he felt. He told me exactly
how he felt, and I could always trust he meant it.

"I'm married."

When Rick finally told me, it felt like a violation of trust.
What if I had gotten pregnant? What if I didn't want to have a
child out of wedlock? I understood why he had hesitated to tell
me. How do you explain when you haven't been dating somebody for very long? *I'm married. I don't even really know the woman
I married; we never slept together. It was arranged so I could stay in the
States; she's my old roommate's girlfriend. And by the way, I just gave you
the power to get me deported.* But then, once you've been dating
somebody for a while, and you trust her enough to tell her, how
do you explain? *By the way, we've been dating for a long time, and
we're pretty close, but just so you know, I'm married.*

It freaked me out.

On another occasion he said: "In my faith the children take
the mother's religion. But you don't have a religion. So if we did
have children, of course we would raise them Muslim."

I didn't appreciate that, either.

And there was another thing. I asked Rick sometimes about
Islam. Once he told me about their end-of-time beliefs, which
seemed to resemble the Christian notion of apocalypse. In the
end of days, Rick said, all Muslims would rise up and kill all non-
believers.

So I asked: "Would you kill me? Would you rise up and kill
me?"

And he said: "I don't know."

"*You don't know?*"

That was a big deal to me.

"How can you *not know?*"

He was being honest.

When I enlisted in the Army as a linguist and told him I might be assigned to learn Arabic, he said I was planning to spy on his people. I believed him when he said that if I pursued a military career, there was no way he could be with me.

When I was in fact assigned Arabic, I announced: "Well, we're breaking up."

And he said, "No, I don't want to break up. I still want us to be together. I'm changing my mind."

During boot camp, whenever I was given permission to use the telephone, I called Rick. My decision to join the military was not just a decision to get away from him. In part it was. I admit that. But certainly not entirely. I hated that we were separated. When I completed basic training, he came to see me graduate. By then he'd grown this really long and wild goatee, and he looked like a cross between some crazy terrorist and a hip college kid. My parents didn't know what to make of him at all.

Everything got really complicated. In the end, once I moved to California, it was my decision to start dating other people that finally broke us up. After that Rick would never speak to me again.

It's hard to have someone with whom you've spent two years of your life, and cared about, hate you and want nothing to do with you.

But Rick was also a big part of my decision to enlist, because he gave me confidence that I could handle the Army. He had *so much* confidence in me. He certainly would have wanted me to do something else. Anything else. But the respect he showed me and the confidence he had in me helped me believe that I was capable of doing something I never thought I could do.

I owe him that. Despite how much he hated what I did, I don't think I could have done it without him.

ENLISTED

There was one more reason I enlisted in the Army. I wanted to prove a former boyfriend wrong. I had dated Douglas when I was eighteen. A real arrogant son-of-a-bitch who wanted to be a Marine, he told me, and liked to yell at me—as if yelling at *me* was good practice for his Marine duty. He'd yell at me about how I could never make it in the military because I could never handle people yelling at me. Anyway, Douglas and I had this very unhealthy relationship that involved a fair amount of violence. I'm ashamed to admit it, but I was pretty into Douglas for a while, and that was hard, because I *hated* how Douglas made me feel—which was weak and vulnerable. I hated that he acted like he knew something about me that I couldn't contradict. Maybe he was right. Maybe I could never hack the military, how could I say for sure? As for the yelling, Douglas turned it into this twisted deal where I was supposed to *like* that he was cruel to me—as a way to prove to him I could handle it. I'm not proud I stuck with Douglas as long as I did, but lots of women stick in marriages far longer where worse stuff is happening. (And that sucks, too.)

Of course Douglas never became a Marine. For all I know he's drunk facedown in some gutter somewhere.

Eventually I got out of town. I returned to college in Bowling Green, and I got away from Douglas in the process. Leaving town has tended to be my way of ending relationships that I otherwise had no idea how to end.

So, five years later, I thought of Douglas when I enlisted. And even later still, during basic training, when I wanted so badly to quit, I thought of him yelling at me. Taunting me how I could never make it in the military. And I'd think: Fuck you, Douglas. And I kept at it—to prove him wrong.

After I lost my job, no one could console me. I just felt shitty all the time. As if someone had torched my house and the arsonist had gotten the insurance money.

In January 2000, in what was still Bill Clinton's America, I joined the Army Reserves to train as an interpreter. The thought that I might go to war was pretty distant.

The reservists I met were actually cool. I was impressed by how smart and well educated they were. Many had already done active duty, and they enjoyed what they did. They also talked up the benefits of enlistment—the cash bonus, the money for graduate school when I got out. It all sounded good to me.

Enlisting meant I would not be geographically stable, but I would be financially stable. This is certainly one big reason that there are so many low-income whites and minorities in the military. There are many reasons to join the Army. But without a doubt it's a great way—leaving aside the whole prospect of getting maimed or killed—to better your career prospects.

I learned that if I enlisted I'd be gone for two years of training. Two years away from my house. Two years away from my life.
It felt like a huge risk.

It appealed to me. It was a risk I was ready to imagine.

I enlisted in the late spring of 2000. I was twenty-three. The
minimum contract at that time was two years active duty; six years
was the maximum. Due to the extensive training for my MOS
(military occupational specialty) as a linguist, my minimum
enlistment option was four years. But four years meant no signing bonus. If I committed to five years active duty, however, I'd
get fifteen thousand dollars cash for signing plus fifty thousand
dollars for grad school. If I signed for six years, I'd get an additional five-thousand-dollar cash bonus. But I understood earning
potential. If anyone imagined I'd settle for five thousand dollars
for one more year of my life, they could kiss my ass. I signed for
five years.

The ride to boot camp at Fort Jackson, South Carolina, was a fair
sign of what was in store. Pouring down rain the entire way,
cramped in this awful van with holes in the seats and holes in the
floor. The windows leaked and the engine rattled.

Basic training. It was like going to the movies when the picture is totally out of focus. Or the projectionist left the image
off-kilter, and the actors' faces are all split in two. And you're sitting there in the middle of a row toward the front. You've got
your popcorn, your soft drink. You're settled. And when the film
rolls you think, No problem. Someone near the exit will get up
and tell the kids at the concession stand to fix the goddamn picture. But no one moves. The audience sits there. Everyone just
kind of adjusts to the situation. Like they squint or turn their

heads a certain way. Deal with the fuzziness or that the actors' foreheads are below their chins. Maybe the movie is *supposed* to be that way?

I understood that basic training was indoctrination. I understood the aim was to break us down and rebuild us into what the Army wanted. But I was not too amenable to the concept.

It was generally frowned upon to challenge our drill sergeants, but I remember in an Army Values class I could not keep quiet. The drill sergeant was complaining about American antiwar activists: "Those damned antiwar protesters don't know anything. They don't understand how wrong they are and how wrong it is that they do that. They shouldn't be allowed to protest." And so on.

So I responded: "The right of American people to say whatever they want is one reason I joined the military. It's one reason I am willing to die for my country. Those protesters are exercising their ultimate responsibility as Americans by expressing their political opinion."

The drill sergeant did not yell at me. I got the impression it caused him to think—if only for a moment or two.

Mainly I found the drill sergeants to be okay. They respected me as a slightly older, more mature soldier-in-training. A lot of the other new recruits had never lived away from home, had never paid a bill on their own.

On the other hand some of the drills themselves were ridiculous. Take bayonet training.

Drill sergeant: "What is the spirit of the bayonet?"

Us: "To kill! To kill! To kill without mercy, Drill Sergeant!"

"What makes the green grass grow?"

"Blood! Blood! Bright red blood, Drill Sergeant!"

We all screamed "Kill!" in unison and stabbed at tires stuck to four-by-fours.

There were other memorable moments. Like learning to throw a live hand grenade. Or the drill sergeant who explained his personal theory about guns and girls.

"Females do better on the firing range," he bellowed at us one afternoon. "You know why? Because females know how to follow instructions. Having never touched a weapon before, they have to pay attention. Like good soldiers should. As for you men? You could learn a thing or two by watching the females learn."

I neglected to tell him I already knew how to shoot. At Fort Jackson I fired a weapon again for the first time in more than ten years. I was surprised; it felt good. Empowering. I liked having a weapon in my hands again.

I felt like a freak until I realized that so many of us were freaks in one sense or another. I found people at boot camp who appreciated the same alternative music I did, and felt the same cynicism I did about fitting the Army mold. The guys in particular were basically good guys, though they gave us females endless shit for the differential female standards on PT tests: *Girls get off easy. . . . Girls can't hack it.*

They had a point. Females got twenty minutes to run two miles compared to fifteen minutes for males. Push-ups: We needed a much lower minimum to qualify; the guys had to do more than twice as many. But guys couldn't bitch if we passed the male tests. That was my response. I was eventually able to surpass the male minimum standard for push-ups for my age group. I also worked hard to get my run to where I'd meet the male standards. Other girls didn't give a shit. They'd argue that our body types were different, that females tended to have strong abs, but we didn't usually have the same innate upper-body strength as most guys. And some guys understood that.

It's poetic justice that of the two people who didn't make it through Basic, one was male and one female. The girl collapsed quietly; the guy lunged for a drill sergeant's throat and had to be dragged away kicking and screaming by Military Police.

There was tremendous variety among the women in my company. I especially admired some of the older women. One African American was thirty-two and a nurse. She was tough, and the younger black women turned to her for guidance. Another woman was thirty-four, with six kids. Six kids—can you believe it? I have no idea why she enlisted. Allergic to the regulation black socks we wore, her feet got so horribly raw and bloody they had to send her to the hospital for a couple of days. But when she returned she finished the final ruck march. She made it through.

The younger girls were more of a pain. One cried and cried, claiming her recruiter said she'd never have to handle or fire a weapon in the Army because she was a female. Said she'd been horribly misled. Was anyone really this dumb? Had she honestly thought the Army would not make her learn to shoot?

Other girls fixated on appearances. They polished and polished their boots until they motherfucking shone. You could see your reflection in them. I never was that kind of soldier. When it came to appearances, I was going to meet—not exceed—the standard. If a sergeant told me to spit-shine my boots, I did it. But I never did it just to do it. Who gave a shit?

I did not see girls bond at boot camp. Sharing a shower head with another girl was no big deal. We got used to it. But require us to share three washers and dryers for nine weeks? "Who's the owner of this skanky thing?" Girls cut in front of one another all the time. Forced into close quarters, we just got catty. Very catty. I really hated living with females.

"I miss my mom." How many times did I hear this from some newly enlisted teenager? Not me. What *I* missed: Rick's arms around me. My strong and sexy man, so smart and tender. So mine. My dogs: Karma's waggy butt, Kinski's soft fur. Pizza and ice cream. Thai food and beer. Wine. Omelets. Popcorn. Television. Cigarettes. Making love. Being naked. Taking walks. Going to the park. Watching movies. Being alone. Going shopping. Taking a hot bath. Driving my car. Swimming. Cooking. Sleeping late. Calling friends. Air-conditioning. Normal clothes. Privacy.

But I discovered at Fort Jackson I could do things I never knew I could do. Endurance, stamina, willpower. You name it. I found I was strong beyond all my prior understanding. I learned what I could do, because I had to do it.

I also learned to follow the Army's rules, whether I liked them or not.

"What are those streaks in your hair, Private?" A female superior confronted me.

"My hair, Drill Sergeant?"

"Your hair, soldier. What are those highlights doing in there?"

"It's the sunshine, Drill Sergeant. It's put streaks in. I used to dye my hair cherry red, but this is my natural color."

She peered to get a closer look.

"Faddish highlights are not allowed in the Army, soldier. Get rid of them. Dye your hair a uniform shade."

"Yes, Drill Sergeant."

I dyed my hair dishwater blond that night.

I moved to the Defense Language Institute in September 2000. Only then did I learn that my score on the DLAB (Defense Language Aptitude Battery) qualified me for a Cat IV language, the more-difficult-language category. As Rick predicted, the Cat IV language selected for me was Arabic. I began my sixty-three-week course and, due to a few additional weeks of break built into the schedule, I ended up living in Monterey, California, until February 2002.

DLI was like a college campus for soldiers. A surprising number were Mormons. Apparently Mormons frequently did missionary work overseas, for which they were required to go through a language-immersion course. A clean-cut crowd that avoided cigarettes, coffee, and alcohol. Not like the rest of us.

Aside from the thirty hours of language class each week, and PT and other training, we had a lot of freedom. For instance, we could drink in our rooms after an initial period when it was forbidden. As a joint-service environment we were also a diverse bunch. There was even one arrogant jerk with a master's in philosophy from Dartmouth.

I'd always been good at school, and DLI was no different. I got good grades and made dean's list each semester. So when I needed to find a way to pay my bills, I was granted permission to get a job outside. I found part-time work at the Borders bookstore in town. I also volunteered for a Big Brothers/Big Sisters program and hung around with a ten-year-old named Ellen. Took her horseback riding. Brought her to the gym with me when I worked out.

———

I also made a close friend at DLI, although it took awhile. Zoe remembers the first time she saw me. She didn't like me very much. It was a Sunday night meeting arranged by the floor sergeant in charge of cleaning the barracks. The floor sergeant's job was to announce the cleaning duties for the week and ensure they were done on time and to standard; we didn't have a janitorial staff. We were our own janitors.

That weekend I'd been permitted to go off post for the first time. When you initially arrived at DLI, you were placed on restriction. This meant you wore your uniform all the time and you never left the installation. But as soon as I got my first day pass, I checked myself into a day spa for a massage and a facial. I had recently completed boot camp, and my body felt completely beat up.

Right before the floor meeting, where we were supposed to talk about cleaning the bathrooms and sweeping, mopping, and vacuuming the floors, I said: "Hey, I went to the spa today. It was so great. They totally pamper you."

Zoe was appalled. She told me later that she'd thought: Who does that bitch think she is? What a snob! Who does that? Who goes to a fucking day spa? And she could not believe I was wearing an ugly green cardigan. (Of course, years later Zoe is a completely different person. Now Zoe *loves* going to the spa.)

The first time I remember her, we were at a party in somebody's apartment. A girl with curly red hair. Tattoos. An expressive face, an expressive voice. I was sitting on top of a dryer in the kitchen. (In military housing in Monterey the washers and dryers were always in the kitchen.) We got to talking. I was getting wasted, so I have no memory of what we discussed. Probably music and men. That's a good guess.

It's unusual for me to pursue a friendship with another woman, but I really liked Zoe. We'd run into each other and talk. Then we started to go to the farmers' market together. We'd buy ourselves flowers and fresh fruit. There was an Indian place in Monterey that sold Indian burritos. (What's a burrito when it's not a burrito? A nan burrito.) We'd have nan burritos together— and talk. I soon came to feel, though not always in the details, that Zoe was like a younger version of myself.

Beautiful and amazing Zoe. Crazy and wild. Small tits. Great ass. Later guys would joke that the two of us put together would make the perfect girl. My rack, Zoe's ass.

She'd joined the Army when she was seventeen. She'd gotten out of high school and didn't want to go to college right away. She didn't see any way to support herself. She knew the military was there. She knew she could get paid to learn another language. So she picked the same job her mom had in the Air Force, only her mom had been a Russian linguist, while Zoe ended up an Arabic linguist.

In my experience people who have family members in the military are more likely to join the military. It just seems normal. In Zoe's case she saw the benefits of a military life. She'd lived in Japan, Germany, England, and Texas. Her mom retired as a master sergeant after twenty years in the Air Force and then went to law school. Her mom did very well for herself. In the military she was able to raise a kid on her own.

Zoe's folks divorced when she was still a baby. Her dad was not around when she was growing up. Like lots of girls with absent fathers, she's had a tough time forming decent relationships with men. Or trusting men. Or even knowing how to deal with men. Like me, she's been hurt. And like me, she's had difficulties maintaining female friendships. She tended to assume that every relationship would get yanked away from her. So if you wanted to stay friends with Zoe, you had to keep after her.

Zoe also wanted to party a little more than I did at DLI. She was still at that stage where she wanted to go out to bars, get drunk, and meet random men. When I was at DLI, that was not something I did too often.

I watched Zoe grow up in the military. When we met at DLI, for example, she wanted to have a baby. Right away.

"Why shouldn't I get pregnant and have a child? Why not have a baby to love and take care of?"

I was adamantly opposed. "No single motherhood when you're eighteen! Not a good idea."

"But my momma raised me by herself in the Air Force, and that worked out well."

She moved away from that position gradually.

So Zoe and I became great friends. And she was the only person who attended my wedding, besides my husband's parents. At the time she was really my only friend.

As the wedding approached, she was supportive.

"You sure you want to do this? Okay, if you want to do this, I'm there for you."

Maybe it was because of Rick that I couldn't quite imagine myself with an Army guy. Or maybe because the DLI guy I had been dating was so damned competitive with me. In any case, I ended up marrying the anti-Army.

It was at Borders that I'd met my husband. He was my manager. A sweet and sensitive civilian who began to urge me to end my Army life. (Especially after we were married and we saw *Black Hawk Down:* I had been assigned to an air assault division, and when he saw the helicopter crash in the movie my husband freaked over what might happen to me in a combat zone. *I* was freaked because the movie made him cry—in public. There were people I knew in the audience. It made him look like a big pussy.)

A few months later the marriage ended. Zoe remained just as supportive.

"You're way too good for Mark, anyway. He's short. He's bald. Trust me. You'll do better."

Would I? I was confused. Not so confident.

Zoe graduated from DLI a few months before I did and left for her advanced individual training at Goodfellow Air Force Base in San Angelo, Texas. She then left Texas the week after I got there. We both knew we were going to Fort Campbell, and we agreed that when I arrived at Campbell we'd find a place and move in together.

"ARE YOU GOING TO WAR?"

"Are you going to war?"

I was already awake and getting dressed at 5:30 A.M. I had just switched on the television when my cell phone rang. An old friend from my high school days. Her voice tight with anxiety. Worried out of her mind. For me.

September 11, 2001. And there they were. The Towers. A stunning Tuesday morning in New York City. How many dead we had no idea. Later that day I wrote in my journal: "Humpty Dumpty falls off the ledge and all the king's horses and all the king's men can't put him back together again. And he's just an egg, right?"

A funereal hush at chow. Formation tense. The post closed. All noncommissioned officers yanked for gate guard duty. We moved to a high-threat alert. In class the television monitors remained tuned to Al-Jazeera and to the Lebanese channel. (That's what total-immersion technique means. No *Good Morning, America* for us.) Totally surreal to be watching this news from Al-Jazeera's perspective.

Suddenly Arabic is the most important language to know in the world.

A guy in tears in the corner said his sister fucking *worked* at the World Trade Center. Couldn't get his cell phone to function, so I lent him mine. When our Egyptian American teacher arrived, he told us that his lovely American neighbor had spat on him as he got into his car to come to work.

My phone returned to me, I called Tariq in Tampa, but there was no answer. I didn't leave a message. What could I say? I was still so angry at Rick for cutting off contact, even though I also sympathized because I knew what troubles he was going to face if this tragedy had been instigated by Arabs. Why didn't he try to call me? Why did he never try to reach me in the weeks or months after 9/11?

Moving around DLI from building to building became a cruel parody of Checkpoint Charlie. Guards everywhere. *Show your ID. Don't leave your bag. What's in the backpack? What business do you have here? Let's see your ID.* As if the next attack might be here—in Monterey.

I would be lying if I said I was completely surprised or shocked that day. Already at boot camp, the people who trained us had been deployed. The First Gulf War. Somalia. Haiti. Kosovo. They'd gone overseas and done real-world missions. Already then I realized I was probably going to go. Somewhere. The longer I was in, the more inevitable deployment felt.

So 9/11 confirmed that reality for me. I already knew who Osama bin Laden was. At DLI we talked about the terrorist networks that existed in the world. We knew it might happen. We knew it could happen.

During class that day, as we followed the coverage on Al-Jazeera, a Marine yelled out: "Kill 'em all! I can't wait to get those bastards!"

We knew he'd get his chance. We knew we all would.

Biddle's roommates. Connelly was twenty-one and a raging alcoholic, but I chose him because I knew he would not be able to form a connection with me. If I went on a date with anyone else, I made clear to the guy I was not going to provide a relationship. It was not going to be intimate. It was going to be casual. I made that very clear.

FTA

FROM SMALLEST TO largest unit, the infantry
is organized like this: team, squad, platoon, company, battalion,
brigade, division, corps, Army. I was assigned to the 2nd Prophet
Team of 3rd Platoon, Delta Company, 311th Military Intelligence
(MI) Battalion attached to 3rd Brigade in the 101st Airborne
Division (Air Assault). Soldiers in the 101st are known as the
Screaming Eagles. (They used to take an eagle as a mascot into
battle with them.) Soldiers in 3rd Brigade (187) of the 101st
Airborne Division (Air Assault) are known as Rakkasans. It's a
name they earned from the Japanese during World War II; it
means "falling umbrellas." That's presumably how the Japanese
saw them as they parachuted from the sky.

I am proud to be a Rakkasan and proud to be part of the
Screaming Eagles. The Screaming Eagles have a great tradition.
I'll be proud of this for the rest of my life. If anyone ever asks:
"What unit in the Army were you in?" I'll be able to say I was in
the 101st and people will know right away what I'm talking about.

"That's Fort Campbell," they will say. "They served with pride
in Vietnam and World War II."

But when it comes to day-to-day life, your team is what counts.

The team is the smallest and most fundamental unit in the military. During any deployment, it is almost always the most important. When you get deployed, your whole life—everything—is intimately bound up with the people on your team. These are the people with whom you live, sleep, work, eat, fight. You know them better than you know your lover or your spouse. You know what music they like. You know what they eat. You know their shitting habits. And you trust them with your life. You have to.

So if there's a problem within your team, it can be extremely difficult.

I was assigned to a team, but the team shifted several times over the course of the next few months. So I and the people I went to war with never really got a chance to know one another before we left for Iraq.

A Korean linguist, Specialist Geoff Quinn showed up from Korea but then left for a leadership development course for new noncommissioned officers. He returned in December as a brand-new E-5. A buck sergeant with no real leadership experience who tended to rub people the wrong way.

When we did the PMCS (preventive maintenance checks and services) on our truck, for instance, he filled every single thing to the top—including the radiator fluid.

I told him, "You don't do that."

"I'm a sergeant. You're a specialist. I don't see why I should listen to what you have to say."

"But you've never PMCSed a truck before. And I have."

Of course, when SGT (Sergeant) Quinn started the truck, radiator fluid burst out everywhere.

And then our team leader got in *my* face.

"Why did you let him do that?"

"Let him? I couldn't stop him! He wouldn't listen to me!"

(One positive thing I can say about Sergeant Quinn. He got better over time. He did learn. It just took awhile.)

So Quinn was no buffer for our team leader's weaknesses.

Our team leader, SSG (Staff Sergeant) Moss, had not been at Fort Campbell when I first arrived. She'd returned to DLI in California for an intermediate Arabic course. So I didn't meet her right away, but I met people who knew her. They'd laugh about her, but I had no idea why.

Then SSG Moss returned. A small woman who looked confused all the time. She immediately made clear how much she loved physical training. She'd burst out: "Hooah PT! Hooah PT! Hooah PT!" (Hooah in this context meaning "Awesome.")

That fall, we practiced our deployment. We loaded our equipment on our truck. Got it weighed. Got it ready for rail-loading. We banded our equipment with metal bands so it wouldn't shift around or fall out. We taped the lights. Simple things. But SSG Moss had a very hard time. She never quite grasped that the bands had to go *around* the equipment and *through* rings on the truck. She banded the equipment to itself or to other equipment.

SSG Moss also thought we could fit more equipment inside a space than was possible. She drew up a load plan and then taped the plan to the outside of our truck. This enabled us to see immediately what was inside. But she never seemed able to gauge proportions accurately; she was determined to fit larger items inside smaller ones.

We gently informed her: "That obviously won't work."

She always responded with the same puzzled answer.

"Why not?"

"Look at it!"

It also worried me when she discussed the fate of her previous truck.

"Cursed," SSG Moss said. "Every time we went on a field problem, that truck got stuck in the mud."

"Who else drove the truck besides you when it got stuck in the mud?"

"Um, no one."

"But the *truck* was cursed?"

"That's right."

"You don't think your driving might have had something to do with it?"

SSG Moss did not make me feel safe at all.

The fourth and final member of our team showed up only in January. Like Sergeant Quinn, Specialist Lauren Collins was a Korean linguist; she came to us directly from her advanced individual training in Texas. Less than five feet tall, she looked like the sweetest little thing.

I have the most vivid first impression of Lauren.

Lauren had been at Fort Campbell for less than two hours when Sergeant First Class (SFC) Fuller chucked a football right at her, missing her face by inches.

SFC Fuller liked to throw footballs at people. No fewer than three times, he hit me in the back of the head. He wanted soldiers to buck up. He wanted us to act tough. Be strong. A lot of people hated SFC Fuller.

"I will kick your fucking ass!" Lauren yelled at him.

Everyone froze. SFC Fuller was three ranks above her. He

grabbed her and started to drag her from the room. We were convinced he planned to kill her. Start beating on her right then and there.

Instead he told her: "I like to push people. Nobody has ever reacted to me the way you did. I really respect that. You've got one big pair of balls."

So that's my first impression of Lauren. One big pair of balls.

I'd had discomfort in my right foot since June, but the Army took its time with a medical diagnosis. Soldiers always attempted to sham injuries. Cry wolf. So the Army tended to stall diagnoses until things got serious.

My diagnosis was Morton's neuroma. In the ball of the foot there are nerve bundles that run and split down into the toes. A nerve bundle in my right foot was inflamed and, over time, the inflammation caused scarring in the nerve bundle.

I was given a choice. I could get immediate surgery and not deploy with my unit. I would probably miss the war and remain nondeployable until I was completely recovered. Or I could deploy and deal with the pain in Iraq with occasional cortisone shots.

I refused to deploy late. I would take the shots and put off the surgery.

Our unit deployed in February 2003. As world opinion spun on its axis away from support for the invasion of Iraq, we spun in the opposite direction—closer and closer to absolute certainty. We would go to war because that was the way it worked. We had signed a contract. We had given our word. It might not mean too much to give your word anymore, but that did not mean we would not keep ours.

For the longest time, though, we kept hearing the same refrain.

"There is no deployment order for the division."

We responded: "Uh-huh. But we are going to deploy?"

"No. There is no deployment order for the division."

"See those railroad cars with our trucks on them? Those cars are going to Jacksonville to get on a boat and take our trucks to Kuwait. That means we are going somewhere."

"No. There is no deployment order for the division."

"Just admit it! Tell us something like: 'Hey, look. We can't give you any dates. We can't give you any specifics. But we all know it's going to happen, so be ready for it.' Just say it!"

"There is no deployment order for the division. But you'd better go get your anthrax shot. Make sure your will is up-to-date. Get a power of attorney. Please update your life insurance policies. Be sure to set up automatic bill payments. Get a smallpox shot. And you females? If and when the order comes, be prepared to pee in a cup for your pregnancy test."

"Quit lying to us! A duffel bag with all our extra gear has already gone to the Middle East. We've been told to pack personal hygiene equipment for six months! We went to Wal-Mart and spent three hundred dollars on binoculars, batteries, cameras, books, and a solar shower! Extra fucking everything! And you're trying to tell us we're not going anywhere?"

"Roger that. There is no deployment order for the division."

Then the deployment order for the division was announced on CNN. It was lunchtime, and everybody's phones all started to ring at once. So we checked it. We went to CNN.com and printed out the web page where it said the deployment order for the

101st Airborne Division (Air Assault) at Fort Campbell had been published.

Our lieutenant came into the office. We confronted her with the news.

"So the deployment order is out."

She shook her head. "There is no deployment order for the division."

"It was on CNN. A major is quoted as saying that the division is getting deployed."

She got flustered. "Well, what does he know? Who's this major anyway?"

"He's the fucking public affairs officer! He's the person authorized to speak to the press for the division!"

"There . . . there's . . ." She stammered. "There is no official deployment order until we've had a formation and had a chance to announce it to you."

FTA. We said it all the time. Some soldiers even took a Sharpie and wrote it on their duffels or their helmets or boots— any damn place they could find. *Fuck the Army.*

A week later I left for Kuwait as part of the advance party for our unit. Zoe drove me to post that day. It was a Sunday. A light snow fell. I had a rucksack and one duffel bag. My second duffel had already gone with our trucks.

We hugged a tearless good-bye.

"Now don't go and start the invasion without us. Be safe."

Except for a brief time in Kuwait, I wouldn't see Zoe again for six months. Until after the war proper ended, and the president had stood on an aircraft carrier in front of a banner that announced: MISSION ACCOMPLISHED.

HOW TO PREPARE FOR DEPLOYMENT TO IRAQ

1. Every night until you deploy, sleep in your vehicle. Or sleep on a cot next to your vehicle.
2. Sandbag the floor of your vehicle as protection against improvised explosive devices.
3. Get your semiautomatic rifle and empty a round into the side of your house. And spread gravel throughout the house and yard. For atmosphere.
4. Find the most annoying alarm sound on your cellphone, and set it to go off at least once each night. At different hours.
5. Arrange for neighbors to wait until you are sound asleep then come outside and beam a flashlight into your face. Have them tell you that there's an emergency but then immediately change their mind and announce it was a false alarm.
6. Hire a garbage truck to run all day and all night in your driveway for correct ambient noise. Keep a pit of manure burning for proper fragrance.
7. Practice being physically separated from your spouse or

your girlfriend or boyfriend. Communicate with him/her only via cellphone, e-mail, and snail mail.

8. Ask two hundred people you don't know and don't necessarily like to live with you for a month. Make sure there are at least five times as many men as women.

9. When it rains, go dig a hole in your backyard. Fill a pail with dirt and stir it with rainwater. Slowly pour this mixture over your entire body.

10. Once you are good and filthy, use baby wipes to clean yourself. Don't take a proper shower for two weeks. Pretend you don't know what you look or smell like.

11. Handwash some clothes in dusty water only. Mix and match them with sweat-stained and torn clothes. Wear the combined outfits proudly when you meet with your boss or go to a dinner party. ·

12. Never clean your toilet and be sure always to urinate on the bathroom floor. Remove the toilet paper entirely. Better yet, walk to the bathroom at a gas station at least half a mile away. Always carry heavy equipment, a weapon, and a flashlight.

13. Whenever you feel you have to pass gas, go to the bathroom "just in case." Every time.

14. Take your once-every-two-weeks showers in public, preferably on your front lawn; pretend not to notice that people are staring when you strip.

15. Only eat food that has been prepared by strangers, making sure that you never have any idea what it is. Or what's in it.

16. If you drink coffee, be sure to let it sit for several hours before drinking.

17. Drink all beverages—including water, milk, and soda—either lukewarm or very warm.

18. Attach a flashlight to the bottom of your cot. Whenever you want to read or write at night, crawl under the cot.

19. Before you use the telephone, have a family member unplug the phone from the wall so there is no chance you can get through. Attempt to make phone calls anyway. Don't let this affect your morale.

20. Tell your neighbors that every dog on the block may be rabid. Gather up the dogs, shoot them, and burn them.

21. Travel in convoys with your neighbors. Drive very slowly, careful to avoid plastic or paper bags in the road (in case they are explosives). Carry your weapon with you at all times. Point it at anyone suspicious. Stop at every bridge and overpass and inspect them for bombs before driving over them.

22. Travel to the most dangerous neighborhood you can find in an up-armored Humvee. Dig survivability positions with overhead cover. Unroll concertina wire in the streets. Establish checkpoints on every block and tell anyone who wishes to pass through that they will have their vehicles searched upon demand. Tell residents that you are there to improve their situation.

23. Detonate unexploded ordnance in this neighborhood in the middle of the night. If residents are upset, tell them not to worry, things are going according to plan. If they complain that their living room windows have been shattered by the blasts, reassure them and inform them that plastic should work fine. Tell them glass windows were too dangerous, anyway.

24. When your child asks for a ball to play with, have him find the precise one he wants on the Internet, type up a Form 9, attach a printout of the web page, put everything in an envelope, mail it to a third party for processing, and tell your child the ball will arrive in just a few weeks.

25. Just when you think you're ready to resume a normal life, do everything on this list again in order to prepare yourself for the unexpected extension of your deployment.

FULL BATTLE RATTLE

OUR ADVANCE PARTY arrived at a commercial airport in Kuwait on February 18, 2003. It was an astonishingly long trip—more than twenty-four hours of travel, from Nashville to Chicago to London and Dubai and into Kuwait. I read an entire book on the way and realized that I might have seriously underpacked reading material.

We were in civilian clothes on civilian flights, so we could drink—which I knew was lucky; the rest of the unit would not have that privilege. They would fly over in full gear, packed on chartered planes, with no chance to soothe their nerves. I had a few beers along the way. The flights looked maybe half military. The British soldiers got drunk. We stood out, even in civvies. Especially the guys, with their buzz-cut hair. When we stopped briefly in Dubai for "security reasons," no one was allowed off the plane, even to smoke. One of the Brits—who had already been chastised for smoking in the bathroom—lost control at this indignity and ended up shaking the seat in front of him, reminding me of a caged monkey.

At the Kuwait airport no one was there to meet us, and we waited several hours before we finally made it through customs and someone showed up to take us to the local U.S. Army base, Camp Doha. While waiting, we wandered the airport a bit, got coffee, looked at shops.

When we were finally loaded into SUVs and on our way, SSG Moss, who had been relatively quiet and controlled on the trip, perked up.

"I'll be running you folks up to Camp Doha," the driver informed us.

"Run?" our team leader interjected. "Will there be an opportunity to run?" I looked across at her, silently pleading with her not to embarrass us.

"I'm sorry, Sergeant?" the driver asked politely.

"Running might get some of these knots out of our necks, you know?" she announced, apropos of nothing.

"We're passing Checkpoint Alpha," the driver said into his cell phone, no doubt alerting someone at the camp that we had arrived and were safely on our way.

Our sergeant was not listening, or not following what was going on, and I was beginning to feel the urge to throttle her. "I'd love a good run," she said to no one in particular. "Won't that be great? When we get there? The last time I was here I ran the perimeter every day. Can you still do that?"

The driver again called in our position. "We're passing Checkpoint Bravo," he said.

"Oh, really?" she answered.

A minute passed and she got it. "Oh. . . ." We all exchanged glances, sighed, and shook our heads.

Camp Doha. A world of sand and grit, thick enough some days to stick between the teeth and cloud the air to hazy white. The sun was incredibly hot. Inside the camp things weren't so bad. They had movies, a rec room, a library, a PX. A good chow hall where they periodically served lobster. My vegetarianism did not preclude my digging into a little crustacean, though I couldn't deal with the removal of its exoskeleton, and asked someone to do that for me.

We trained on new equipment for a few days before we pressed on to Camp Udairi. The amenities were fewer out there, but it was still pretty comfortable. There were tents with cots to sleep in, trailers and showers a ten-minute walk away. Larger tents served chow. In general, though, there were simply fewer distractions from the mission to come and the unpleasant thoughts that crowded in.

Waiting. That's all this was. Waiting. There was no doubt in our minds that this war was on. Time was the only variable, the only question mark. Not if, but when.

We heard reports of the worldwide protests against the invasion and the war. It was hard to know how to feel. I was positive that some of my civilian friends were among the protesters. And *of course* I didn't want to be here, either. The thought that I might possibly die in the desert . . . and for what? For whom? I was here because of my loyalty to my unit and my fellow soldiers. That was the beginning and the middle and the end of my sense of loyalty at the moment. That was what mattered. That was what kept me going: hoping I could make a difference; hoping I could provide good intelligence that saved even one life.

At the end of February we headed out to a site near the Iraqi border for three days of pulling live mission. We were living in more primitive conditions—not even Porta-Johns out there, just "field-expedient" shitters. These involved a toilet seat bolted to a chair frame and a plastic bag. It worked remarkably well. I was impressed by the ingenuity. The unit with which we'd been training also had generators, a luxury we appreciated for the heaters they powered; it was still cold at night.

My first sight of Iraq was a hill in the distance with a tower on it. Through binoculars we could see the Iraqi soldiers near the tower, no doubt looking back at us looking at them. We were teamed with a SECFOR (security force), infantry boys in their Bradleys, all ready to get out of this limbo and into combat. They were from Third Infantry Division (3 ID), out of Fort Stewart, and had already been at this site on rotation for a few months. On the drive there and back, I studied the landscape. The hesitant patches of green on the desert, from a distance like hints of stubble on a man's chin, but closer up looking like patches of mange.

Things were remarkably quiet. Under the circumstances, you could say it was spooky how ordinary life was. For the most part we were each left to our own thoughts while not on shift. Not that we had privacy. It was a given that someone could amble over and talk—about this, about that, about nothing. Mainly you took it for granted. Sometimes, though, it could get pretty strange.

"Hey, Specialist."

It was one of the 3 ID guys. I was bored, so I didn't mind the company.

"Hey," I answered him. He was a mechanic, a good guy so far as I knew, just someone everyone liked to joke around with.

"Y'all having a good time yet?"

"We're ready to end all this waiting. And just go. You ready?"

"Ready?" He cast me a big smile. "We're ready for anything. Bring it on, I say."

There was a little bit of an awkward silence then. But I was still feeling basically fine about the chatter.

"You know, my wife," he started, out of nowhere. "My wife and I, we like to do it hard, if you know what I mean?"

"Excuse me?"

"We like it rough, if you follow me? The rougher the better, so far as she's concerned, and who am I to complain? It works for her, it works for me."

Had I said or done anything to indicate I wanted to hear any of this?

"Yeah," I said, but I'm thinking *no.*

"Like if she were here right now," he said, then stopped. "Let me put it to you this way. She's not here. So I'd love to break the back axle of that Humvee there on you. If you get my drift."

"Uh, I'm sorry. I'm not really interested."

"I'm just saying," he said. "We see you girls in your T-shirts. We can see your boobs. You know we're watching."

I walked away.

Later on I seriously reflect on whether guys actually believe that talking to girls like this *works.* Or whether it's some kind of obnoxious ritual, some kind of compulsion to say anything—like dogs feel the need to piss on a tree and call it their own. Must guys say everything that comes into their pea brains when they're feeling horny—or whatever? That is, if what this guy was feeling was horny. I'm not so sure. Granted, we were on the edge of war and all that might mean. Sure, it must have made some folks do or say crazy things. But was that an excuse?

After the three-day mission, it was back to Camp Udairi. I developed heat rashes between my legs and on my waist. Itchy inflammations—bug bites?—sprouted on my ankle. Blisters appeared on the arches of my feet where the sand got inside socks and shoes when we ran. We had to carry our gas masks while we ran, which was worse. The rubbing and chafing of the weight could only be offset by gripping the mask when you moved. But that meant you couldn't swing your arms as you ran, and you lost rhythm as a result. I was realizing fast that being deployed was like being in the field: You had more time to focus on your body, its functions and complaints.

In the tents where we worked, shifts in the wind pushed the sides so it felt as if we were on a boat. Watching the shifting walls of the tent move somehow tricked my inner ear.

Insatiable thirst marked each day. All you could do was attempt (and fail) to quench it with water that also tasted like dust.

Sand stretching into vastness. A harsh, stark, desolate kind of beauty. The distance clouded always by dust, dust, dust. I wondered if there were names for the different types of sand, like we have for different types of snow or rain. There was the sand that was packed firmly, and that must be slogged through. And there was the sand that was delicate like confectioner's sugar or flour, so powdery you sank in and it billowed up in puffs when you stepped into it. There was fine blowing sand that misted your face lightly, and harder granulated blowing sand that stung when it hit your face.

Oddly, though, it was all almost relaxing. There were no bills to pay, no phone calls to answer, no friends or family to see, no daily chores to mind, no shopping to do. Daily life was nothing like *real* daily life, and while this was no vacation, it was also not so bad, either.

———

In early March the rest of my unit arrived in Kuwait, and we joined them at Camp New Jersey. It was very similar to Camp Udairi—sleeping in large, open cloth tents, with segregated male/female sleeping areas. There was a lot of down time. People played a lot of cards. The weather kept getting hotter, and it became so oppressive that all you wanted to do was lie still.

Our vehicles, shipped over on boats, finally arrived a couple of days after we got there, and we bused down to the port to drive them back. We were given a convoy brief prior to the drive back, detailing the route, speed, and rules of the drive. During this brief I noticed movement behind me and turned. A soldier had a nosebleed and was stanching it. No big deal. Glancing down, I saw his blood on the sand. The brilliant red stood out so much against the bland beige, I couldn't help but stare. *Please,* I begged silently. *Let this be the last time I see blood on sand.*

When we were trying to link up with the Kuwaiti police escort that would accompany our convoy back, I was called upon to translate. And found myself horrified at the deterioration of my Arabic skills since I graduated from DLI. It had been almost a year since I left Monterey, and there had been no language training at Fort Campbell. (For many of us this had been a big concern; language is such a perishable skill. There should be a mandate that military linguists and interpreters continue to receive language training at their permanent-duty stations.)

We stopped at a checkpoint, and I needed to ask the police manning it where the police escort for our convoy was. I was reduced to asking, "Where are the police for us?" since I couldn't remember the words for "escort" or "convoy." The cops must think I'm stupid, I thought, when I asked them, "Where are the police?" Just hearing and using the language, though, started to bring it back. We linked up. Nonetheless the experience still left me nervous about my language skills, and fearful that I would be useless.

Having our vehicles and equipment gave us more to do, getting everything prepped. Practicing, packing, seeing what would work now that we knew exactly what we had to take. The number of DOS (days of supplies—of food, water, batteries, and so on) we had to carry kept getting bumped up—five to seven to ten—necessitating several reorganizations of our gear. At least we were doing *something*.

The chow tents were a few hundred meters away, and long lines formed before they even opened. They were open for breakfast and dinner; lunch was an MRE (meal ready to eat). The food was typical for institutional dining. A small shopette run by AAFES (Army and Air Force Exchange Service) in a trailer was stocked periodically, and sold out almost immediately of the items people most wanted—cigarettes and pogey bait (civilian food).

There were occasional sandstorms. It became hard to see as painful grit pelted the eyes. One evening the blowing sand got so awful that some people put on their gas masks to shield their eyes and ease breathing while walking back from chow.

On March 12 we moved to full battle rattle. Everything on (or carried) all the time. In case of attack we needed to be prepared.

Kevlar: a flameproof lightweight fiber first developed to reinforce the tread of radial tires. Our soft Kevlar flak vests protect the upper body, the shoulders, and back, and are sewn together inside a nylon shell. There are supposed to be ceramic bullet-proof plates that slide into pockets in the front and back of the vest, protecting the heart and lungs, but the majority of people in my unit never had these. (There simply aren't enough to go around, so those considered more likely to be in high-risk situations get them.) A vest without plates can stop bullets from handguns and fragments from mortars and hand grenades. A vest with plates can stop bullets from high-powered rifles. In addition many of us had a load bearing vest (LBV), if we had old-style equipment. (As I did.) This held our ammo pouches, canteens, and so forth.

The Kevlar vest weighed nine pounds without plates. Add a four-pound Kevlar helmet, and we were already thirteen pounds of gear, plus mask, weapon, and a basic load of 210 rounds of ammunition. We also carried, in a bag, our joint-service lightweight integrated suit technology, or JSLIST (pronounced just *J-List*), that is, the suit that was going to protect us from biological and chemical attack. It was particularly frustrating in the chow tents, too much gear in too little room. A high-ranking officer was quoted as saying that carrying all our gear "improved morale." I thought this was crazy.

In my Kevlar helmet, I carried a medevac card so I knew how to respond in case someone in my unit required a medical evacuation. I carried a casualty feeder card in case I was seriously injured or killed in battle. (I was instructed to fill out the personal data on this card, but I couldn't bring myself to do it. I was superstitious about this detail.) I carried a copy of the ROE (rules of engagement). I carried a code of conduct (first developed when Eisenhower was president) in my Kevlar in case I was captured as a prisoner of war.

I memorized the code of conduct:

I am an American, fighting in the forces which guard my country and our way of life. I am prepared to give my life in their defense. I will never surrender of my own free will. If in command, I will never surrender the members of my command while they still have the means to resist. If I am captured, I will continue to resist by all means available. I will make every effort to escape and aid others to escape. I will accept neither parole nor special favors from the enemy. If I become a prisoner of war, I will keep faith with my fellow prisoners. I will give no information or take part in any action which might be harmful to my comrades. If I am senior, I will take command. If not, I will obey the lawful orders of those appointed over me, and will back them up in every way. When questioned, should I become a prisoner of war, I am required to give only name, rank, service number, and date of birth. I will evade answering further questions to the utmost of my ability. I will make no oral or written statements disloyal to my country and its allies or harmful to their cause. I will never forget that I am an American, fighting for freedom, responsible for my actions, and dedicated to the principles which made my country free. I will trust in my God and in the United States of America.

I believe it was John McCain who said that the code of conduct helped him get through his time as a POW.

On the band of my Kevlar, I also had my blood type written. Our blood type was on our dog tags, but a lot of soldiers also wrote it on their T-shirts and their boots. When you enter a combat zone, you think to put it everywhere. (All soldiers know their blood type.)

We also should have carried forms in case we confiscated

enemy equipment. And we should have had forms in case we took prisoners. But no one I knew had those forms at the beginning.

At full battle rattle we ran drills periodically in which everyone huddled into the back of a MILVAN, which resembled nothing so much as a metal truckbed. (Officers got into concrete bunkers, where, I imagine, they had a higher chance of survival.) The story was that a MILVAN would protect us, either from incoming rounds or from chemical attacks, but this appeared quite unlikely. If a MILVAN took a direct hit, having us all together meant that the enemy would kill us all at once. We also put on gas masks while standing inside these metal containers, so it became extra uncomfortable and difficult to breathe.

The whole thing would have been completely insane if it hadn't also been incredibly real.

Specialist James Reid was not on our team, but he was in our platoon. He joined us at Fort Campbell almost immediately before we deployed for Iraq, so no one knew him real well. He was always very laid back and calm. Quiet. Quirky. Funny once you got to know him. I always felt as if I got on his nerves because I could be so intense and excitable much of the time.

If I was happy about something you'd know about it.

"Oh my God, the sunset was so beautiful! You totally should have seen it! It was so cool looking!"

Or if I was mad, you'd know about it too.

"I can't stand that fucking bitch! I hate being around her! I'm so pissed off!"

But Reid always stayed cool.

"Yeah," he'd say, real slow and calm. "Yeah, she can be a real pain sometimes. I don't know about her."

That was about as demonstrative as he ever got. In the course of an entire year in Iraq, I never saw Reid lose control.

Later, once we got to the mountain site, some of the soldiers got to calling Reid "Lawyer" because he'd gone to law school and passed the bar in Kentucky. Having no interest in practicing law, Reid had joined the Army and ended up a Korean linguist who, like Sergeant Quinn, came to us direct from a year in Korea.

But calling Reid "Lawyer" was not a disrespectful thing. Everybody liked him.

So sometime after we go to full battle rattle, Staff Sergeant Moss, Reid, and I pull guard shift together from 2400 to 1200 hours. Our straightforward task is to watch the ammo dump. It's too easy.

"Be at the vehicle at 2345," SSG Moss tells me.

I'm there. She's a no-show. I'm tired and impatient and I'm thinking maybe she means *Zulu time*. Whatever. I head back to bed. At 0010 she comes to get me.

"You're late," she says in a supersnotty voice. "Get Reid and meet me at the vehicle."

I keep the peace and say nothing. I just get my gear together and go outside so I don't wake everyone up.

"Let's move, soldier," she says.

I stare at her.

"Can I put my gear on first?"

"I don't want to hear any attitude," she says, giving me truck-loads of *her* attitude.

We get Reid, and the three of us move to the perimeter and settle down for the night. Reid and I locate positions for the night, leaving SSG Moss in the Humvee, which she randomly moves about five times, reparking it. At some point I swear I hear her talking to herself in the truck. Weird. I light a cigarette. Finally she gets out of the truck and comes over.

"You'll have to move," she says, pointing to my cigarette. "Twenty meters away from the ammo. A precautionary measure." She turns and starts to go. Then turns back again. "And come tell me first."

"Come tell you what?"

"Williams," she says. "Watch your attitude. I've already asked you once. Don't make me tell you again."

I throw the cigarette down into the dust, too tired to deal.

"Sergeant," I say as calmly as I can. "I'll just sit here and stare at the ammo. Okay?"

"And change the way you're sitting," SSG Moss says. "I've been watching you. Leaning down on one hip like that. Shifting back and forth. Our platoon leader could come out here and think you're drifting off. Not paying attention."

I stare at her in disbelief. She's criticizing the way I *sit*? But I maintain control.

As the night drags on, SSG Moss never leaves the vehicle. Not once. Every hour we have to make reports to the battalion tactical operations center (BNTOC), and I expect the three of us to rotate this chore. Foolish me. SSG Moss says Reid and I will make the hourly fourteen-hundred-meter round-trip walk together. This we do—eleven times—with full battle rattle. Adds up to more than fifteen klicks (that is, fifteen kilometers) of walking.

My foot problem was horribly painful, more so when I had to

carry weight. As a good *soldier,* I sucked it up and did what I was told. As a good *leader,* Sergeant Moss should have remembered my problem and considered it. After all, we had a damned truck!

But SSG Moss never relieved us, never made the walk, never used the vehicle provided. Just bitched now and then about the shitty detail. Somewhere in there she tells us she's got a headache and could we go farther down to pick up some Motrin for her?

When it's time for breakfast, SSG Moss orders that we can't go for hot chow. We could leave the prescribed route for her needs but not our own. When our shift comes to an end, a captain from BNTOC arrives and tells us we're done for the day. Incredibly, she makes us walk one last time back to BNTOC to confirm that this is accurate information. Ridiculous! I am so angry and hungry I want to bury my head in my hands and cry in frustration. When the shift finally does end, that is exactly what I do, alone and secretly, on my cot.

IN-COUNTRY

MARCH 21, 2003—the day before the invasion. We were back at Camp Udairi, linked up with the rest of our GAC (ground assault convoy). Tomorrow, Iraq. No time to think about that, though, with alarms going off repeatedly, all day, all night. Three quick car horn honks signaled an al-Samoud missile overhead—gas. A little unnerving. Seven seconds to mask up, in case our Patriot missile missed the al-Samoud. The masks stayed on until we heard the all clear. Problem was SSG Moss never seemed to notice it. We took to demasking without her authorization. Then at some point she'd suddenly yell at us to demask, apparently oblivious that we already had. Was she going to be this slow the entire time we're deployed?

Saturday, March 22. I entered Iraq for the first time, in the second vehicle in the 4th GAC of the 101st Airborne Division (Air Assault). We were behind the Army's Third Infantry Division, which had left for Baghdad on Thursday night. We stretched endlessly across the desert, averaging between fifteen and twenty-five kilometers a hour, like the most intense traffic jam in the world.

It went slow. And it stayed slow, and hot, and mind-numbingly dull. Drive and drive and drive. I saw no resistance. We were advancing, and we would keep moving as long as it took to get to FARP Shell (our forward arming and refueling point)—at least two days of near-constant driving.

My weapon was loaded. My mandatory protective gear was on. But there was no resistance. Nothing at all. We saw burned-out vehicles on the side of the road, damaged buildings—but weren't even sure if these were from this war or the First Gulf War.

My team was lucky. We GACed with 101 Aviation, which meant pilots were in charge. Pilots were more laid back than other commanders. So a couple of times we were able to stop for a few hours; drivers were allowed to sleep. The pilots gave us extra batteries and T-Ration waffles, a welcome break from MREs. There was an embedded reporter in the lead vehicle, Colin Soloway from *Newsweek*. He was very bright, an engaging conversationalist, and highly knowledgeable about the region: talking to him was a real pleasure. We had an electric outlet in our vehicle that he used to charge his satellite phone. In exchange he let us call home, and gave us hot water made on the one-burner camp stove he'd had the forethought to bring. It was a little thing. But in this kind of situation, a little thing was incredibly important.

Then there was SSG Moss. She messed with a key piece of equipment and somehow busted it. "Oops," she said, the vital piece in her hand, "I broke the card in the computer." We had been repeatedly instructed never to touch the card, so I asked: "Why did you touch it?" "But you *can* touch it," she replied. "Yes, but they instructed us not to," SGT Quinn said. "But you *can*," she insisted.

This continued for a few minutes, obviously in vain. The air grew tense in our Humvee. We tried to raise anyone from our platoon on the radios, to get a message relayed back for a replacement. But we couldn't get through at all.

"The vehicle in front of us," I volunteered, "they've got a satellite phone. We could call in."

"I don't know," SSG Moss said lethargically. We continued to try the radios. She ate and chatted with people around us.

Luckily, during refueling, we found a tech able to do an emergency repair job and got our system back up.

That wasn't the end of Staff Sergeant Moss's unpredictability. She drove the Humvee erratically, pressing too close to or staying too far from the vehicles in front of and behind us. We could barely stand to watch. She wouldn't let Lauren drive since she didn't have a military driver's license, and we agreed that SGT Quinn shouldn't drive because his vision was so bad. He didn't have the plastic adapter to hold his special glasses inside his mask, so if we were chemically attacked and he had to mask, he'd be driving blind. So I drove almost the entire way across Iraq, while Quinn sat beside me working the radio, and SSG Moss in the rear seat running ops (operations).

Outside the scenery changed from dust and sand to green and greener. Not at all what I expected. The second day we were back to dust and sand.

Stops to go to the bathroom weren't pleasant. On the first day, we females opened the doors on one side of the vehicle and hung up a poncho to create a little privacy. But this didn't last. The poncho went first, and not long after, any hint of modesty. You just dropped your pants and squatted with your butt toward the truck on the side with the fewest people. Of course the guys pissed everywhere—or they went behind sad, straggly bushes to take a shit. It became impossible to care. How could you? Stops sometimes lasted fewer than five minutes, even though getting in and out of chemical gear took forever, especially with three chicks taking turns because you were also pulling security. Some guy getting a random peek at my butt quickly became meaningless.

Iraq was not just a giant cat box, as we called it. We also turned it into a garbage dump, leaving a vast trail of trash in our wake. We littered our way through southern Iraq and this brought out the locals, who were friendly and supportive—but also very hungry.

Those days we drove through small villages, and locals lined the streets, cheering for us. Curious and unafraid, the men and kids came right over to the slow-moving convoy and made their demands known. They wanted food. We'd been instructed never to pass an MRE out the window while we were driving, but it was tough to resist their pleas. These people clearly supported the invasion. And we were wasting so much food. Whenever we stopped, protocol demanded that we burn what we left behind. But Lauren and I sneaked a stack of MRE meal parts we wouldn't eat near a pile of trash. It was crazy to be here supposedly to help—and then not help those who needed it most.

Food. We all spent a lot of time in Iraq thinking about food. I certainly did. Of course it's tough to be a vegetarian if you're living on MREs. True, there are twenty-four different varieties, but most of them are entrees like Meat Loaf, Jambalaya, Country Captain Chicken, Thai Chicken, Hearty Stew with Beef, and Boneless Pork Ribs. Yes, there are vegetarian meals: Pasta with Vegetables and Tomato Sauce, Pasta with Alfredo Sauce, Cheese Tortellini, and Bean and Rice Burritos. But in Iraq you couldn't always get the meal you wanted. In fact, since the meals came in two different cases, twelve to a case, you could keep getting one kind of case over and over. That way you not only didn't eat what you preferred, you were also starved for variety. Sounds like a small thing, but over time, especially wartime, it takes on huge significance. Truth is, you'd be bumming after a while. Us, we kept getting Case A, Case A, Case A, Case A, Case A. So there would be these times we'd come across some other unit, and we'd get to talking. "We only ever get Case B!" they'd say. Time to trade. Doing a drug deal, we called it.

All over Iraq, soldiers did drug deals. You name it, it got traded. Once we swapped batteries we found on the side of the road with another unit for some maps. They didn't have batteries. We didn't have maps. And we constantly traded MREs. Big prize: a Lorna Doone shortbread cookie, or M&M's. When I'd get one of these treats, it would be awesome.

It totally pissed our team off when Staff Sergeant Moss *ratfucked* our cases of MREs. That's what we called it. She'd rustle through MRE after MRE, looking for the one that had the Lorna Doone. It drove us nuts.

Another unpleasant thing: MREs were essentially a fiber-free diet. Nothing accidental about that—the military wanted to stop you up, so you didn't have to go to the bathroom as often. Less interference with your ability to do your mission. And that was fine if you were in the field for a few days. But it became problematic if MREs were all you were eating for months—which is what we did. Possibly every MRE had fruit in it—diced pears in heavy syrup, or diced peaches in heavy syrup, or apple sauce. But an MRE *never* had green vegetables. Never. Fruits are full of sugar that give you an instant rush of energy. But green vegetables don't, plus they have almost no calories. So what's the point?

Over time we tried some MRE experiments. We learned to mix and match. I really liked to mix the minestrone stew with the mashed potatoes to put together a half-assed version of shepherd's pie. I'd go through our box of extras—the remains that others had not wanted to eat—and pull out the things I wanted. Keep in mind that maintaining my vegetarianism, which I was determined to do, meant there was very little I could eat. I was desperate. So I got creative. For instance, I couldn't eat the Mexican rice because it had beef stock in it, but I could eat the beans. I couldn't eat the Thai chicken, but I could eat the white rice it came with. So I'd mix the white rice with the beans. But no ingenious mixing and matching made up for the fact that there were only two vegetarian MREs in a case of twelve. That meant one out of six MREs was vegetarian, and I was one out of four people on a team. Even if I got every single vegetarian MRE, it would still not be enough for me. And in fact, I tried to be cool and polite, and took whatever was there. If it turned out not to be a veggie MRE, then I'd eat what I could from it—crackers and peanut butter or crackers and cheese. Then I'd put the remainder of my meal in the box for the others to dig into, and take what I could out of the box to supplement.

On Monday the 24th, we made it to FARP Shell. That was when we were hit by a tremendous sandstorm that lasted three days. The wind whipped the dust upward. The air grew thick. The sky turned a sickly orange and then suddenly almost black—so dense you could barely see. Within minutes dirt clogged up everything. Worse, it was in your eyes, your hair, your mouth. We couldn't sleep sitting upright in the cramped seats of our vehicle, so we finally fell into the back of the truck next to us, our exhausted bodies weirdly entangled, an arm here, a leg thrown there. It was dark and cold, and we listened to the crashing of the wind and sand, felt the truck shake. But we slept. When we woke, the dust had coated every orifice that was at all moist—eyes crusted shut, lips and nostrils caked in grit, and tongue and throat coated with a film of dirt. It was horrible.

Rain began to fall. We hoped it might weigh down the dust, or rinse off the filth. But when it started to beat on the windshield, we saw it wasn't water, it was mud. It was raining mud. By the time the storm ended, our green vehicle was brown. There wasn't even a thought of washing ourselves—water was rationed.

There were no showers. No rinses. No way to get this off you other than the ubiquitous baby wipes. I hated the smell of them. Staff Sergeant Moss used the scented variety; the rest of us used unscented. But either way the wipes didn't do a lot of good; you rubbed the spots that got dampest or dirtiest—groin, armpits, feet, hands—every chance you got. But it was a losing cause. You moved on. And you tried not to feel more than the absurdity of it.

But the awfulness of the filth paled next to our team leader's critical errors in judgment. Leaving her flak vest lying around when she left the area. Not donning her JSLIST top but bitching at me if I took mine off. Leaving her ammo rounds unsecured outside the vehicle at night. We didn't speak for days, except when absolutely required. And when we did speak, I would not stand at ease with her, even at her order. I told her: "Sergeant, I believe it is more appropriate for me to maintain military bearing with you at all times."

There was nothing she could do about it. I was demonstrating that I would respect her rank, but that was all—the ultimate show of *disrespect*. When she tried to open a conversation about my attitude, I shut it down. I knew that I could not be faulted for my bearing, since it was completely correct.

So there was little conversation. No one wanted to break the tension, so it festered. We all withdrew into our own personal shit, talking less and less, at least when she was around.

I considered all over again how someone like SSG Moss managed to become a noncommissioned officer. The military system puts everyone up for promotion after a specified period of time unless there is a paper trail flagging problems. In SSG Moss's instance her college degree, her motivation, and her enthusiasm for PT gave her points; in all other areas, she merely had to demonstrate passable skills and show proper military bearing. Which, apparently, she had.

Our shifts were six hours on, six hours off, staggered so that I had three hours with Sergeant Quinn and three with Lauren. This meant that there was always an Arabic linguist on shift—and that SSG Moss and I never had to work at the same time. But I was getting just three hours of sleep at night. During the day, with the temperatures above a hundred degrees and the sun blazing, it was almost impossible to sleep. Exhaustion was making me increasingly irritable.

After eight days, which felt more like five weeks, Lauren and I managed a solar shower with two precious bottles of water each. We rigged a poncho and got naked behind it—in itself a rather wonderful experience. I managed to wash my hair and body, and even though I scraped off only a top layer of crud, it still felt great.

———

From March 30th to April 5th, we colocated within FARP Shell with Alpha Company, 1st Battalion, 187th Infantry (1/187). They took good care of us, gave us supplies our unit had not been able to get. Lauren and I were big coffee drinkers, and they let us share their "cowboy coffee," made in big vats with the grounds stirred right in. Strong, gritty, but hot and good. Some of the guys almost fell over laughing as Lauren and I tried to dig a survivability position. We're both pretty small, so our survivability position was supposed to be approximately thirty-six inches deep (unlike a foxhole or fighting position, which would had to have been deep enough for us to stand in). But about a foot down we hit a thick, hard layer of salt. It had to be broken up and then removed, along with big rocks. Luckily the guys decided to show us how it should be done, and what strong men they were, and they did it for us. A rare moment when I took advantage of the benefits of being a girl.

By this time, I could already tell the difference between the smell of burning trash and the smell of burning shit, a skill I never really had the desire to acquire. The latter is more acrid, stinging the eyes and burning the nose. We burned our shit soaked in JP8 diesel fuel throughout our deployment. (And soon I learned that the smell of dead animals being burned is another smell entirely—the worst of all.)

One day I tried to use a military phone to call home. I spent an hour trying to get through, failing miserably. It was frustrating and upsetting, and I ended up wishing I had never tried at all. In this emotional state, I got lippy with SSG Moss, and then retreated into my shell of protocol.

"We can't do this," she says. "I need this to stop."

"What are you talking about?"

"You don't communicate with me. You lock up every time I approach you. I want this to stop."

"Yes, Sergeant." My eyes straight ahead. My posture stiff and proper.

"At ease, Specialist Williams."

But I am not moving.

"Williams, *please*—"

Is it happening? Is that what I think it is?

Staff Sergeant Moss is crying. It isn't anything huge. Just a tear or two. But I see it, though I might not have noticed if I weren't studying her.

The bitch.

She's crying in front of a subordinate, and I have even less respect for her now, if that's possible. You *never* cry in front of a subordinate. Especially if you're a woman in a position of authority. The guys already think we can't handle this. It just isn't done.

I don't say a word. Not a word. She stands there for a moment, a single tear running down her cheek.

Then she turns and goes. I should feel guilty, but I don't.

Later that day, our platoon leader, Lieutenant Malley, came over. She pulled me aside to talk.

"Specialist Williams, I know that you are not doing anything to Staff Sergeant Moss that anyone can fault you on," she told me. "But what you're doing is really hurting her feelings. And really, you should relax and try to be normal with her because it's getting hard for her to cope. It's getting out of hand. You can't go on like this. You really need to back down. Relax."

LT Malley was smart and efficient, if highly strung. She was someone I understood. A lot of people didn't. Later, she became our company's executive officer (XO), and she was great at it—very organized. But as a platoon leader, she'd micromanage like a motherfucker, and that was tough on a lot of soldiers. As a West Pointer, she also didn't trust noncommissioned officers. I've heard rumors that at West Point they actually teach officers not to trust NCOs.

Just because an officer attends college doesn't mean she knows shit about the Army or how things really work. So many West Point graduates have little real-world experience. They live in dorms for four years and then go straight into the Army, never having had a job outside, never having rented an apartment, never having had to be responsible or having to take care of themselves on their own.

So for instance here was LT Malley, West Point and two-and-a-half years of Army experience, and our platoon sergeant—with his seventeen years of experience—was technically serving under her. Guess who really knew what the fuck was going on?

One time, at Fort Campbell, when we were getting ready to go to Iraq, everyone was doing a million things at once. We were always frantic and rushed. We'd be at work from 4:30 A.M. until 8 P.M. Then the order came down to paint the bottom of our A bags and B bags tan, and then stencil them black with our last name, the last four numbers of our social, what unit we were in, and so forth. The bottoms of our B bags had to be done that day. I carried them outside to paint them, then went back in for a moment to get another bag. When I returned, LT Malley was sitting there, crouched in the parking lot. Painting bags.

"Ma'am, what are you doing?"

LT Malley was tense as hell.

"They said these had to be painted by eleven o'clock!"

Calmly I said: "I think I can handle it."

"But it has to be done!"

Again calmly I said: "Ma'am, I know I'm only a specialist. But I think I can manage painting some bags." Admittedly I was being a bit of an asshole here. "So why don't you go inside and do whatever it is that you do that makes you deserve so much more money than me."

I actually did say this. It was an inappropriate way for me to talk, but it jarred Lieutenant Malley. She looked at me. She took it in. We'd spoken off-line before, casually, a couple of times. So we'd already established that she understood I was competent.

"Okay. You're right."

I said I understood LT Malley because I'd had experiences not so different from hers. When I was twenty-two and working in Tampa, I had an assistant, but I was so young that I had no authority over her. If she showed up late, there was nothing I could do about it. It was an awkward position, and probably because this was my first job with real responsibilities and I was so young, I got extremely emotionally invested in what I did. If I made a mistake and something went wrong, I took it very much to heart.

So here was LT Malley in what was most likely her first job after college. She was twenty-three or twenty-four years old, and she had a platoon of over twenty soldiers she had to lead into combat. Combat. We might get chemically attacked. Some of us might die. Before we went to war, there were estimates of 30 percent casualty rates. (No official statistics: just rumors. If the Iraqi army had actually stood and fought, rather than run away, who knows what might have happened?) So LT Malley was looking at her soldiers and thinking: I'm in charge of them. I'm responsible for them. They might die right in front of me.

That had to be overwhelming. For someone who's a perfectionist, that had to be very tough. She wanted to do everything herself. (I'm not so different.) But as a leader, she had to learn to let other people do their jobs. She had to delegate responsibility. I knew it would have been hard for me.

So we understood each other. She pissed me off, but we could talk. We talked a bunch of times. And so on that day in Iraq, we talked about SSG Moss, my disgust with the situation. And Lieutenant Malley actually commiserated. Inappropriate for both of us, but she convinced me. Helped me see that my stubbornness was hurting the whole team. Also—to be honest here—I felt I'd won something. I'd proven my point, in a sense, and that freed me to bend. Some of the tensions eased, and SSG Moss and I started working somewhat better together.

We're pulled for a mission with Division, and get briefed. Then we're sent out into the field with other teams. Finding units in the field ought to be a no-brainer, but there's little coordination and poor planning. Our four-digit grid coordinates are vague at best, accurate only to within a square kilometer of our target location. Under these circumstances, it's amazing we find the first two locations. We drop a team at each site.

As we drive through random Iraqi villages, we see that it may not have been the best idea to send MI teams out without infantry support. We have only the most general sense of where we are going. A few hours later, we're lost. The town we are driving through is the same town we've driven through twice before. The same locals are sitting and watching us go back and forth. They're looking a little puzzled. What are those Americans doing now? It was a damn good question. We later heard rumors that this town had seen a few ambushes of American convoys. I am so glad I didn't know this at the time.

Locals come out to look at us. Waving white flags (as in "Don't shoot me" or "Go America," we can't be sure). Giving us the thumbs-up. Always the thumbs-up. The people we see seem so happy. Waving and smiling and pumping their fists in the air. But at the same time I recognize pro-Saddam graffiti on some of the buildings, though no one comments on the disconnect. Mainly we are relieved that the people appear to welcome us. Not hate us.

We go on. Suddenly they're waving dead white chickens.

None of us has ever encountered anyone waving a dead white chicken. None of us knows what it means. Are they offering us something to eat? Are they making an obscure reference to something about Americans, the United States, our invasion? Is it a gesture of resistance or of mockery? What the hell is going on?

I'm not talking one dead white chicken. Or ten. Or fifty. As we continue to drive, we are seeing locals waving dead white chickens *everywhere*. And now that you mention it, we are seeing dead white chickens in the road and on the roadsides by the hundreds. We drive and drive, and there are thousands of dead white chickens.

But that is not the strange part.

The strange part is that we have been trained how to recognize a chemical attack. And one of the first signs of a chemical attack is dead animals littering the roads. And so we consider the scenario and we ask ourselves: Should we suit up? Don our chemical protection gear? Are we under chemical attack?

But the locals are absolutely unfazed. They are smiling and laughing as they wave the dead chickens. That's the first problem. The second problem is the perfectly healthy-looking black and brown chickens scampering in our path. If this is a chemical attack, it has killed only the white chickens. The nonwhite chickens are all fine.

Has the evil dictator of Iraq devised a racist chemical weapon that only kills *white* chickens?

Soon someone on our team starts to laugh. And then we're all laughing. Laughing hysterically. Why? That's hard to explain. But there's something so blatantly bizarre about this situation. So manifestly hallucinatory. We don't feel threatened. We know we are not the target of a chemical attack. Just a cosmic joke. And given the scheme of things—our fatigue and frustration at having gotten so utterly lost—it's a huge relief.

A couple of weeks after the dead white chickens incident, the *Newsweek* reporter traveling with our unit does some independent research. He thinks he has an answer, and it's nothing like what we expect. Turns out that one of Saddam's sons, Uday or Qusay—no one can say for sure—had a chicken factory where he liked to breed white chickens. With the invasion, the factory had been abandoned by soldiers sympathetic to the regime, and the locals had overrun it. They'd decided to take out their anger at Saddam by releasing the chickens into the wild where—bred for captivity—they had no survival skills. And promptly died by the thousands. The locals, wishing to demonstrate their enthusiasm for the U.S. troops, waved the chickens to demonstrate their hostility to the toppled dictatorship.

Thousands of dead white chickens on the roads or not, we're still lost and frustrated. Soon the sun starts to set. We wander aimlessly back and forth on various roads through anonymous towns. We have no maps.

The sky is going dark, and this is nuts. A handful of MI soldiers with small weapons and no combat support in the middle of Iraq in the middle of an invasion. What *was* the plan, exactly?

We eventually locate an infantry unit that has dug in around an abandoned building by the road. A berm has been built for protection, and after being in the truck all day, it's nice to stand up and stretch, walk around a little.

They don't mind sharing their space with us, but they ask that we share guard duty. It sucks since we've already been on twenty-four-hour operations. But it's fair. We're posted around the perimeter and lie on the berm, peering out into the darkness.

We've got NVGs (night vision goggles), but no mounts on our Kevlar helmets, so we hold the goggles to our eyes with one hand while we grip our weapons with the other. When we squint through the goggles, everything goes luminescent green and black, a kind of shadowy glow is cast over everything. Occasionally, and over time, fatigue sets in and the mind plays tricks. Is that a bush? Or a man? Staring through NVGs all the time gets tiring, and there's some moonlight, so we switch back and forth. We're a little paranoid. Howling dogs roam everywhere all night long. Are we supposed to communicate with any suspicious person or persons, or are we supposed to shoot on sight? The rules of engagement aren't covered often, and we weren't briefed on any specifics that night.

———

In the morning, without much sleep, we press on. Continue the search for our location. Before too long we find the unit with which we are to colocate, pick a site, and resume a regular shift schedule for operations.

I see local women in the distance, and I watch them through my binoculars. A number of women collect sticks and carry them in bundles back to homes that lack windows and roofs. A few other women lead donkeys and carts piled with stuff. It's all so ordinary. An ordinary day for them, despite the war.

Before sunset, though, we learn that the other unit is not expecting us to spend the night. And might not let us stay.

"*What?*" We are incredulous.

Their commander gives no ground.

"I repeat: No one cleared this. We will need to check with higher about this."

"What do you expect us to do? Go drive around in the dark?"

"Just stand fast until we figure this out."

None of this inspires confidence in anything other than the certainty of military incompetence. Like death, like taxes, military incompetence is something you can bet on. (You know the World War II saying, right? *Snafu*—situation normal: all fucked up.)

After a while it gets straightened out. They let us stay.

Here's the good part: While we're with this unit, I discover halal/kosher meals.

I'm walking around and talking to infantry guys when I notice a case of them.

"What's that?"

"Those are kosher meals. No one wants the fucking things. We don't know what to do with them."

"Can I look?"

I open one or two, and I cannot believe it.

"Can I please have these?" I start to beg.

"Yeah, get 'em out of here. They're just in the way. We're tripping over them."

The vegetarian MREs I've been subsisting on provide carbs but no protein (except for peanut butter—and how much peanut butter can a person eat before feeling ill?). But these halal/kosher meals, all pork-free and approved by both Jewish and Muslim authorities, are amazing. In each case of twelve there are six vegetarian meals. I score two cases—a dozen veggie meals total. They actually taste good, and they are made with real food! (When I read the ingredient list, I know what everything is. "Chickpeas," "tomatoes," "flour," "water," and "beans," instead of whatever artificial ingredients are in the regular MREs.) All the accessory packs have real sunflower seeds and peanuts and raisins. It is all so much healthier. And the accessory packs also include black pepper, which is very exciting. I never used to like pepper, but it is a flavor I really grow to appreciate during my deployment.

Up to this point I've been getting fewer than twelve hundred calories a day, even though I need at least two thousand. After this, at least for a while, I am able to eat one halal/kosher meal almost every day. But it's still not enough to maintain my weight. I have been losing weight—a lot of weight. But now for the first time since I've been in-country, I don't feel like I'm starving.

"Halal meals? You are not authorized to have them." My platoon leader goes on: "The chaplain has said that there needs to be a religious reason."

LT Malley is following a precise rule, and not watching out for a soldier in her command. This infuriates me.

"I'm not getting enough protein." I hate trying to explain this to her.

"I can't make these sorts of special arrangements—"

"I'm not asking for special arrangements." I try to keep cool. "These meals are out there. And no one is eating them. They're getting thrown away, mostly."

"I'm sorry. I can't get these meals for you. And the chaplain agrees. You're not Muslim. You're not Jewish. I can't make these arrangements for you just because you have a personal preference—"

"I'm not—"

"What if every soldier decides she wants some special food?"

"Ma'am, I don't think—"

"Is that all?"

"Yes, Ma'am."

Later, I mention my problem to our supply sergeant. She says: "I can get you halal meals. No problem." It takes her twenty minutes to get me two cases.

So why the fuck could our supply sergeant do this, but our platoon leader couldn't? She has the rank. She could have gone to any supply sergeant and said: "I need these now. Put them on my truck."

Because in Iraq, doing the right thing isn't always the right thing.

Because Lieutenant Malley, like the good West Pointer she is, fucking followed the rules. You cannot always do that.

When I arrived in Kuwait, I weighed 140 pounds. Over the course of the next several months, I lost more than 25 pounds.

———

On April 8, a Tuesday, we got sent out with an artillery unit. We were finally realizing that we were going to get tossed around from unit to unit on a regular basis. It was frustrating never to get really comfortable with anyone, but it was simultaneously cool and interesting to see how a variety of units operated.

Pulling operations while artillery is being fired is not easy. My job is listening. Artillery is *loud.* Even though these were relatively small guns—105mm—whenever they fired, that was all I could hear. And if I was sleeping, it woke me without fail. I was amazed when I was on shift once and watched SGT Quinn sleep through a lengthy barrage. He snored. The closest gun was less than ten meters away!

While we waited for the convoy to get ready to leave, I met a local who wanted to talk to me—in Arabic—about the invasion. Tanks were rolling by his house, and there was an entire arty (artillery) unit parked in his backyard. He wasn't pleased. His children were scared. He wanted peace and freedom, but not this way. He wanted the U.S. Army to get out. What could I say? I'm sorry? I *was* sorry. *Maybe things will get better,* I told him. But I still felt pretty damn helpless. I left a bag of Skittles for his children— the only offering I had. I think this offended him even more.

Lauren may be the other girl on our team, but we didn't exactly strike up a warm friendship. Not at first, anyway.

She's careful around SSG Moss, and careful around me for disrespecting SSG Moss. So we're polite but have little to say to each other. Mainly, if we talk at all, it's to rag on Sergeant Quinn, since he's way too innocent. Like a lot of people, he wears his Birth Control Glasses in combat, but they look awful on him. We call them BCGs because these big thick plastic Army-issued glasses are so ugly; our thinking is that nobody will have sex with you if you're wearing them. I certainly avoid mine. (I figure if a chemical attack fuses my contact lenses to my corneas, it really won't matter if it happens moments before I die.) Lauren and I learn pretty fast that Quinn's probably never even slept with a girl, and once we get a good laugh when we tell him we've probably kissed more girls than he has. But he's too stiff to laugh, or smile, much. His promotion still sits uncomfortably on his shoulders.

Things change after our first direct encounter with small-arms fire. We're back with an artillery unit, just getting settled, and when we first hear it, I don't register immediately what it means. *Pop, pop, pop!* My first thought is: That sounds like the firing range. Then it clicks in my mind: They sound like gunshots because they *are* gunshots. The guys in the artillery unit take cover behind their vehicles.

We're slower to react, but SSG Moss, Lauren, Quinn, and I take cover in the dirt behind the vehicle on the side opposite the small-arms fire.

As I get my bearings, I realize the danger is pretty far off. We can't see who is firing, and are behind a lot of our own guys, so we wouldn't dream of shooting back. It's best to wait.

"Get up, Specialist Williams!" It's Staff Sergeant Moss.

"What?!"

She's facing me in the dirt, from behind the other tire.

What the fuck is she talking about now?

"Get in the truck and run ops." This sounds like a ridiculous order. She wants me to get in the truck, put on headphones, and start listening for enemy communications. I look at Lauren and she meets my eyes. In an instant I see that Lauren is getting it at last. *What is wrong with this woman?*

"Get up and go pull ops, Williams!"

I ignore this. It cannot be happening. NCOs are not supposed to make their soldiers do anything they won't do themselves, so I think she can get up and pull ops herself if it's that important. I watch the combat-arms guys, figuring I'll get up when they do. They're better trained at this than we are.

I am pretending I can't hear SSG Moss, and I look away. The enemy fire sounds weaker, ever more distant. The threat lessens with each passing second. But I am not moving. I am not going to stand up and walk around for no reason until we are completely safe.

"*Oh,*" Staff Sergeant Moss says with an odd emphasis, as if realizing belatedly why I stayed put. That the bad guys have been shooting at us, and our best strategy is to take cover. Follow the example of the artillery guys we can see.

I try to read her face, but there's a blankness there, a stunned incoherence that I don't understand at all. What is she experiencing at this moment? Is she afraid? Does she know that asking a soldier under her command to get up and move around to get into the vehicle while we are under attack is stupid? Or what the hell is going on? Is she trying to get me killed?

For what seems like the hundredth time since we've been in-country, I ask myself: How do people like SSG Moss survive in the world? Or let's put it another way: How am *I* going to survive working for this woman?

Two days later, traveling north with the same arty unit, we came to a site near Babylon, the ancient city on the Euphrates River.

We stopped near a statue of King Hammurabi, whose dynasty ruled this region almost six thousand years ago. We passed the area where the Tower of Babel supposedly stood. A lovely area, it was a tremendous relief after so much time in the desert.

We took a trip to one of Saddam's presidential palaces, a gigantic building with immense rooms, two elevators plus a service elevator. Each room had its own distinct design, with its own elaborately painted ceiling and its own chandelier. We'd never seen anything like it, and once we reached the balcony and looked out onto the huts below, we were blown away by how this splendor existed in the midst of outrageous poverty. The people were beyond impoverished. And every day they got to look up at *this*.

Near the palace I assisted a few American reporters as a translator so they could conduct interviews with locals. They let every soldier use their satellite phone for five minutes. I attempted to call my father and mother in the United States. This felt huge, and I got very excited. I'm at war in Iraq, and I'm calling home. When I got my mom's voice mail, my excitement turned to anger. Not at home? When I got my dad's voice message, I sank even further. Did I really expect them to be sitting around the telephone on the off chance I might call?

A few local boys joined us in the palace, and they latched onto Lauren and me. Asking us in Arabic if we had boyfriends, if they could be our boyfriends, or if the soldiers with us were our boyfriends. Clearly trying to puzzle out our relationship to this military situation. We laughed at them, and I joked with them, but even I had to admit that these boys reeked. It wasn't their fault; there was no running water in these villages. But still, I felt a little uncomfortable. Uncomfortable as well that I was having these feelings. Not wanting to fall into the attitude so many soldiers had about Arabs—that is, that they're smelly, awful people.

Once again Lauren and I filled a box with MRE remains—the stuff none of us wanted to eat—before we left, and I labeled it "nutritious food" in Arabic for the locals.

On the highway to Baghdad a disturbance brings our convoy to a halt.

Word comes down that the unit in front of us has come under small-arms fire. Usually you just push through, but the whole series of convoys has ground to a halt. We're at the tail end, and our instructions are to hold traffic. No one goes forward. No locals pass through. Everything stops.

Lauren and Quinn are Korean linguists with technical skills to do signal intelligence, but no Arabic-language skills. That leaves SSG Moss and me to deal with the language issues. I see the crowd gathering, and a handful of guys working to keep them in place, and I jump out to help.

Everywhere I've been I've made signs on MRE cardboard boxes saying, STOP. AMERICAN MILITARY CHECKPOINT. ENTRY FORBIDDEN. Made flashcards for guys manning roadblocks. Drilled people on basic phrases in Arabic. It's my duty to help whenever I can with my language skill—the Army paid for me to learn! So this is just another way for me to contribute.

"I'm not doing this," SSG Moss says. "You talk to them."

She's acting like it's a block party that's gotten unruly.

For the first hour or so the locals are understanding when I tell them that there is danger on the road and they can't move forward. They are interested in me, this blond girl speaking Arabic, this girl in the Army—I am an anomaly, a distraction. I

105

keep putting them off: "Another half hour, God willing." It's a great phrase, one that they generally accept. It's out of my hands, all up to Allah.

After a while, though, coming from the north on the highway, other locals are telling those folks we have stopped that there is no problem, the road is safe and clear. The crowd grows. And it continues to grow.

Even though we have weapons, the people don't want to listen or respect us any longer. I tell them over and over to stay behind the rear vehicle, but they push forward, again and again.

"It's too dangerous to pass! *Dangerous!* Please listen! We'll let you go through as soon as it is safe to move!"

I'm almost alone out here with the crowd, there are maybe six guys with me, and I'm the only one who speaks Arabic.

Except SSG Moss. I run back to the Humvee.

"I seriously need help," I tell her. "Someone else who speaks Arabic to explain what's going on."

"I told you once," she says calmly. "I'm not talking to these people."

SGT Quinn tells me that the first sergeant also told SSG Moss how much we needed her help, but she refused to get out of the vehicle.

The crowd is getting more frustrated, with men pressing closer and starting to intimidate me. I'm not scared, exactly, but I'm stressed. And I'm wondering whether I can kill my team leader for leaving me to deal out here by myself.

I'm yelling now. Starting to get angry. And then I have an idea.

I go get Lauren.

Now Lauren is a tiny person. She's perky and cute, and

speaks with the gentle twang of someone from a small town in Texas, which is where she's from.

But she's tough when she needs to be. And she backs me up.

Did I also mention she's the one on our team with our most serious-looking weapon? It's an M-249 squad automatic weapon (SAW). This is a big gun capable of firing 750 rounds per minute. When this little woman with the stern look and the dark shades moves to my side and holds her SAW up for everyone to see, there's a real hush in the crowd.

This weapon says: *Respect me.*

Lauren sets it up facing them, and everyone makes a nice neat line behind the rear vehicle. I grin at her.

Soon enough the road opens again. And we move on.

AT THE MONASTERY

BAGHDAD. April 2003.

Our team settled into an abandoned compound, a sort of manufacturing plant, with 1st Battalion, 187th Infantry (1/187). There were military guards with guns sitting at the entrances to the compound; no one got in or out without passing a checkpoint. No locals were permitted on the base. Lots of big buildings with office supplies. Bathrooms were a hole in the floor and a spigot. But there was running water. Spigots lined the main road. When Lauren and I walked to the aid station, several dozen infantry guys were stripped naked in the street to wash at the spigots. We laughed and waved. They looked embarrassed. Then they laughed and waved back.

I am asked whether I would be willing to go out on missions with the infantry. They have no civilian translators. Translation is not my job, so I do it almost as a favor. In part it's better than just sitting in the compound. It's a chance to see the local area, meet the people, and experience the immediate results of my work. Though it is certainly *way* outside the realm of my official responsibilities.

Why else do I do this? Think about it.

Put yourself in the position of some eighteen-year-old infantry soldier with a loaded weapon in a country surrounded by people who don't speak his language. And these people come up to him and yell. They want to tell him something. And he doesn't know what it is. They might be saying to him, *I love you, and I am so glad you are here to liberate my country.* Or they might be saying to him, *I'm about to fucking kill you.* So this kid is eighteen and he's got his loaded rifle—and he doesn't know *what* they're saying.

In the Middle East, people have a different communication style than Americans do. Americans have this three-foot-space rule. We do not want anyone to invade a space within three feet of us when we talk. For most Americans this is standard. In the Middle East the space is much less—it's more like a foot or six inches. They get right up in your face. And they will yell. It looks to most Americans like aggression. But it isn't. It's friendly.

This is something I had to get used to while I was dating Rick. I watched him interact with his friends, and I often thought they were about to fight all the time. But they were having this casual friendly conversation.

No doubt my experiences with Rick gave me more sympathy, understanding, and respect for the people in Iraq. For starters I never looked at them as having some freakish or weird religion. I didn't look at them as being foreign. For me there were things that were comfortable and comforting about being around Arabs. I spent a long time with Rick and a lot of time with Rick's friends. So I acquired a familiarity with Arab men. Things that might offend other Americans about Iraqi men didn't bother me. Like how close someone got when they talked to you. It didn't upset me.

109

But there was something I did realize once I got to the Middle East. When I had been with Rick, his friends never looked at me sexually. They always treated me with total respect. So at the time I just thought Arab men were very respectful of women. But when I flew into Kuwait and walked around the airport in my civvies, these Kuwaiti men were staring at me. A couple of them followed me around. I was horrified.

"You're not allowed to do this!" I wanted to tell them. "It's against your religion. You're supposed to be respectful!"

That's when it hit me. Rick's friends' respectful and polite attitude toward me had *nothing* to do with their culture or religion. It had nothing to do with me. It had everything to do with Rick. They were being respectful of *him*—not me. They were showing him respect by showing respect for his possession. *Me.*

But my having known Rick did help me in Iraq. For one thing I never told locals that I learned Arabic because I was Military Intelligence. I never said I spoke their language so I could spy on them.

Locals asked: "How come you know Arabic?"

I said: "Because my ex-boyfriend is Palestinian."

Or I said: "Because my boyfriend is Palestinian." (This had the added benefit of making me "taken," and it prevented local guys from hitting on me.)

Either way I had some Arabic dialect from knowing Rick, so it was easier for people to believe me. It helped me feel safer saying I knew Arabic due to Rick—rather than saying I'm Intel. At times it could be difficult because there have been tensions between the Palestinians and the Iraqis. After all, here were a miserably poor people whose president was giving money to the people of another country. (Saddam Hussein gave "martyrdom bonuses" to families of Palestinian suicide bombers.) Still, my language skills and my ability to speak about Rick made things a whole lot easier for me. For the most part, locals treated me well.

One day in Baghdad, our platoon leader ripped Quinn a new asshole right in front of us. Our first sergeant was present. Our XO at the time was present. And Lieutenant Malley came up, and it was obvious something was wrong. You could tell.

"Sergeant Quinn, get out of the truck this instant! Get out of the truck and stand at parade rest!"

So she was screaming at an NCO in front of us, and I was lower enlisted. That's not appropriate. If she had a problem with a noncommissioned officer, she should have taken him aside. You do not hem him up in front of his soldiers. How was I supposed to respect him if I had to watch him getting hemmed up?

So we were all frozen, watching this. But that was how LT Malley was. For instance she'd come up to me when something got fucked up, and she'd start yelling at me about it.

And I'd be thinking: Don't yell at me about something being fucked up. I can't make these people do anything. You want to yell at me? You want me to be in charge of this shit? Promote me and put me in charge.

I'd say: "I'm not in charge. You can't talk to me about this. There's a noncommissioned officer right there. Sergeant Moss is right there. Sergeant Quinn is right there. You'll have to talk to one of them. Don't look at me. Don't talk to me."

We clear a school.

We've all heard the stories of Saddam and his army stashing

weapons in schools and mosques. Places we wouldn't attack without provocation, so we know that even these places must be searched. This is my first chance to see how the infantry works. I hang back a little. Stay out of the way. Wait until I'm called.

The school is a group of buildings inside a walled compound. I linger near the entrance with the radio guy, doing some loose crowd control—basically chatting with locals, doing my bit to be friendly and "win the hearts and minds." The children especially are fascinated by an Arabic-speaking, blond, female soldier. One little girl offers me a rose, and I hold her in my arms while her father takes our photo. I wear the flower in my flak vest all day.

Before too long a call comes over the radio to send in the linguist. I am directed inside to "three women" and asked to translate. One woman is hysterical and terrified. She carries a baby and holds a small girl by the hand.

"What is the problem?" I ask her as I am told to do. "Are there weapons in this school? What is your position here?"

She tells me she is a teacher, and that she knows nothing about weapons.

"I am afraid," she says between sobs, "of the men with guns."

She has no Intel value. She fears for her life and the lives of her kids. With the commander's permission, I lead her out of the compound.

"Don't be afraid," I tell her. "No one will hurt you. We're here to help you. Don't be afraid. Everything is fine."

Once we get outside, she runs crying into the arms of her mother. I try again to soothe her. Her family thanks me, and I return inside.

I move with the infantry guys as they clear rooms in the school.

We come across an older man, his wife, and their two children. He says he is the guard of the school, and that his family lives on the premises. He points to pallets of bedding on the floor.

The daughter is making bread when we find her. Her hands covered in dough, she wipes them on her clothes. She is desperately shy and will not look at me.

We gather the family together all into one room. I ask the same questions I asked the teacher.

"Are there any weapons here? Have you been asked to hide caches of weapons?"

The father begins to complain of chest pains.

It's all we need. Have this man die of a heart attack in front of his family.

"Medic!" I call out to the soldiers. "Get a medic for this guy!"

It takes awhile, but we calm him down. It's only an elevated pulse. Nothing serious. A couple of ibuprofen as a placebo, and he begins to breath normally again.

His grateful son voluntarily leads me to one old Soviet-era rifle his father has to guard the school.

I thank him, but he expresses concern that his father will get fired when he reports his gun missing. I write out a receipt in Arabic and in English that says the U.S. Army has confiscated this rifle. There are proper forms for this, but I don't have them. So I use scrap paper. It will have to do.

We clear a military compound.

It looks like a joint Iraqi/Palestinian training facility. There are paintings everywhere of the Iraqi flag and the Palestinian flag. There are posters glorifying the first Palestinian female *sha-*

113

heeda (suicide bomber). There is also a MOUT (military operations on urban terrain) site, for urban combat training, and an obstacle course. A couple of the rooms have UXO (unexploded ordnance), and a couple of rooms have been deliberately destroyed. I go through files looking for papers that may be worthy of DOC-X (document exploitation). There are files of Ba'ath party members and soldiers. I take a few training manuals, one on PT/hand-to-hand combat, one on weapons. We look over posters that explain how to fire a rocket-propelled grenade, and others on chemical warfare. Eventually, some civil affairs/psyop (psychological operations) guys show up, and they bring a civilian interpreter with them. I show him around, but I am extremely confused when he picks up the few unburned files on women and tears off the photographs, leaving the papers behind. He shows no interest in the men's files or photographs.

We clear a monastery.

I know on some level that Iraq has a small Christian minority, but finding this monastery astounds me. It certainly explains the many people in the neighborhood who ask if we are *mesihi*. Christian. It is a Catholic neighborhood—*catholiqi*.

We are in an area of Baghdad called Dura. It is quite lovely— trees, orchards, homes inside walled compounds. The doors, as in most of Iraq, are elaborately designed and often blue.

We go in the back of the compound. The grounds are lush, well tended and groomed. Around to the front of the building, which is beautiful and clean to a degree that is surprising. Amazingly the UN embargo and the ravages of two wars have somehow spared it.

We knock, and a man in robes ushers us inside.

In Arabic I repeat my by-now-standard questions.

"We must search this building. For weapons. Do you have any weapons here? Or caches of weapons and ammunition?"

The monk is polite. He smiles. He responds in English.

"We have nothing to hide," he says. "I am happy to show you our church. However, some of the rooms are locked. The man with the keys is leading prayers in a small room. There." He points to his right. "Perhaps you can search those rooms later? When prayers are done."

The lieutenant in charge of this mission is looking at me.

I look back at him.

We are all silent for a moment.

"Specialist Williams," the lieutenant says.

"Sir?" I respond, uncertain.

The monk stands there, a model of serenity and calm.

"What did this guy just say?"

I glance at the monk, but his expression does not change.

"He says they are in the middle of prayers, and the man with the key to the locked rooms is leading the prayers. When they finish prayers, he can show us the locked rooms."

"Oh," the LT says. "Okay."

But I can't take this.

"He's speaking *English,* Sir. You can ask him anything you want."

The lieutenant is uninterested in hearing my views.

Is it possible the lieutenant cannot understand the monk—simply because he *looks* foreign?

"Ask your commander," the monk says, still in English. "Ask him if he would like to join us. In an Easter prayer. Or whether his soldiers would like to join us in prayer."

"What's that?" the lieutenant asks. "What's he saying?"

"He is asking whether we would like to join them in prayer. For Easter."

"Yes," the monk says brightly. "Today is a holy day. Are any of these soldiers Catholics? Would any of the soldiers like to come and join us in prayer?"

"Huh?"

"He's asking about prayer. Whether any of us would like to join them in prayer."

A few soldiers shift restlessly, almost longingly.

"Can we, Sir?" one of them ventures.

"No!" the lieutenant says loudly. "No. We're at war. We have a mission to do."

I feel slightly sickened. These are Christians in a Muslim country. Haven't they been persecuted enough? Are we really spreading freedom and democracy to the Middle East by clearing this Catholic church?

"We can't wait," the lieutenant says. "Tell him we plan to begin searching the building. *Now.*"

"We could also offer you tea?" the monk suggests. "While we wait for services to end."

I don't even bother to translate this, expecting the usual response from the lieutenant.

"I'm sorry. We can't wait," I say to the monk. "We need to search the building now."

The monk nods, but I can see he is not pleased by this.

So we begin to move through the monastery to verify that everything is clear.

We start down a hall, and the lieutenant impatiently jiggles each locked doorknob. We reach an unlocked door that opens to reveal stairs.

"Ask him where these stairs lead."

"To the basement," replies the monk. "A storage space."

It appears to me, though I cannot be sure, that the monk has chosen to enunciate his English more slowly. As if he is speaking to a child.

The lieutenant rolls back and forth on the balls of his feet.

"What did the fellow say?"

I catch the eyes of a few of the soldiers standing around us. Some of them are also half smiling at the absurdity of the situation.

"To the basement," I repeat.

We go to the basement, where there are precious sacred icons. The only lights provided are the tactical ones attached to soldier's weapons.

There is a room filled with vats of sacramental wine. The smell, heavy and sweet and fruity, hangs in the air, cloying. None of us have had alcohol in a couple of months. We are stunned with desire for it. We move past this room quickly, unable even to articulate our desires to one another.

In the back there is a plywood sheet nailed against the wall. The edges look glued. This draws the lieutenant's instant suspicion.

"Ask him what's on the other side of this."

Wearily I repeat the question to the monk.

The monk nods.

"It goes to the outside."

"It leads to the outside."

"Hm." The infantry lieutenant thinks this over. "We are going to have to break it down. Tell him we don't believe him."

I repeat this to the monk, who is already shaking his head.

"Look," the monk says, pointing upward. "There's a window

to the outside. You can see that this door leads to the outside. There is nothing on the other side of this door."

I repeat this to the infantry lieutenant, who ponders things for a moment.

"No," he finally says. "Uh-uh. Tell your buddy here we are going to have to break it down."

"Please," the monk says. "Send some of your soldiers around to the outside and have them knock on the other side. We'll hear them. And then you can know that this door leads nowhere. It goes outside."

When I repeat what the monk has said, the lieutenant agrees. He sends two soldiers around to the outside.

But he remains suspicious.

"Ask him why this door is barricaded like this. Why did they block this door?"

The monk is becoming agitated. He doesn't wait for me to repeat what he already understands.

"We put it up in case of chemical attack. To keep gas out. This was our way to protect ourselves from a chemical attack."

This sounds too strange and sad even to me. But locals have lots of strange ideas about chemical attacks. I begin to repeat everything to the lieutenant.

"He believes that this plywood would protect them from—"

"Get in here," the lieutenant gestures to the soldiers who have joined us in the basement. "Bust this thing down! Now!"

It just feels wrong to desecrate this place.

By the time they've busted a few holes in it, soldiers begin banging on the door from the outside.

"Yeah," we hear them saying. "It's the outside! Like the priest said!"

We leave the basement and search the simple kitchen facility. We poke into a few of the rooms. Everything is disappointingly empty.

Returning to the foyer, the LT is pissed. The prayers continue. The head monk with the keys has not concluded the service.

"Ask him again if they have any weapons."

I speak Arabic this time.

Dejectedly the monk acknowledges—also in Arabic—that they do.

"We have one AK," he says quietly. "One Kalashnikov."

This is an ancient weapon at least thirty years old.

"And twenty rounds," he continues. "We have twenty bullets."

So that is how the monastery protects itself. What stands between the monks and the looters is one pathetic weapon with its twenty rounds.

I tell the LT about the rifle. He looks absurdly satisfied with the news.

"Find that damn rifle," the lieutenant says. "And confiscate it."

The monk retrieves a key and produces the weapon and its twenty rounds. As the rifle and the ammunition are removed from the monastery, the monk practically begins to beg.

"Please," he protests gently. "Please. We need this rifle. We need to be able to defend ourselves. We have the only computer in the entire neighborhood. And we have religious relics. Please. Everything will be taken."

The LT is slightly amused.

"What was he planning to do with the AK anyway? Shoot an armed mob?"

"Scare people away," the monk insists. "Not shoot people. *Never.*"

I know the LT's orders are to remove all weapons from mosques and schools and organizations. But orders can be interpreted. His orders at this point also stipulate that families can keep one weapon for self-protection. To protect themselves from looting. This lieutenant can make a personal judgment call on this. He can interpret his orders differently—if he wants to.

Again: The right thing isn't always the right thing. The right thing doesn't happen. Perhaps to justify this colossal waste of time or perhaps because this is an institution (and not a family home), the lieutenant is unmoved when I repeat the monk's plea. On the contrary, he takes his actions further.

"It's time to finish this," he tells me. "Tell him we are not going to wait any longer for those prayers to end. They're taking way too long. Tell him to get the keys for those rooms that are locked. We need to search everything. *Now.*"

So during Holy Week we cut mass short. We march into the room where the monks are praying. We order them to return to their rooms and open doors for us.

In this way we finish clearing the monastery.

We find nothing else.

As we pack to go, the monks gather at the front of the monastery. They see the lieutenant toss their AK in the back of the truck. He doesn't bother to glance back. Orders his men to climb in. The job here is done.

I linger as long as I can. I want to say something. Anything. But I can't think what to say. We are abandoning these poor monks to a fate I cannot imagine. I can only hope their building is considered too insignificant. But news travels. No doubt our search has been noted on the street. The word is out: The monks have been disarmed. I give them until dusk—maybe the night—before some gang or other comes busting through their door.

How does this qualify as liberating the people of Iraq?

I load up with the men. Looking back, I see the monk I've been translating for turn away from us, as if we are already gone.

It's over. We're out of here in a swirl of dust.

I never see those monks or that monastery again.

Maybe I told a captain I knew what had happened. How we had stripped these defenseless men of their one rifle. It would be a dramatic breach of military authority for anyone under these circumstances to *return* a rifle to the Iraqi people. Given the circumstances—that we are currently at war—what would it mean to provide a weapon to Iraqis? In plain cold terms, it would be a serious breach of military protocol. There would be *consequences*.

I don't say this happened, but it might have happened. The captain I told about this incident at the monastery headed out there later that day. He arrived at the monastery. Climbed over the back fence. Knocked on the door. Probably interrupted their evening prayers. The same monk came to the door, thinking: Now it begins. But also thinking: Looters do not knock. So he opened the door, expecting the worst, but was then confounded. It was an American captain. Silently and without ceremony the captain displayed an AK rifle. Not *the* rifle. But a good facsimile of it—some other crappy weapon confiscated in a sweep of some other poor soul's miserable dwelling. Hastily the captain handed the AK to the monk.

And he was gone again, even before the monk could thank the captain for this priceless gift.

THE EXPLOSION

EVERYTHING GOES in alphabetical order in the Army. So Alpha, Bravo, and Charlie are dismounted units. They are the true grunts or foot soldiers who, as the cadence goes, "hump it on [their] backs." Meanwhile Delta Company has the mounted gun trucks. There's a good-natured rivalry between grunts and D Co guys. The foot soldiers say the gun-truck guys are "soft." D Co insists that grunts take too long to get anything done—which is true. Dismounted troops always have to get loaded onto LMTVs or civilian buses to get anywhere. Delta guys are often the QRF (quick reaction force). They go everywhere on short notice, and so when it came time to decide which unit should get my services, that's the argument they made. They were the ones who needed a translator most.

So D Co was the unit I frequently got to work with. Often they were accompanied by a combat-line unit, so I met a lot of Joes, but I was closest to the men in Delta, 1/187.

It turned out that I loved working with the infantry. During my year in Iraq those men in D Co were the single best group of soldiers I met. Their commander was a stand-up guy, honest, straightforward, and tough. A man who inspired loyalty. A leader who made you want to try harder and do better. He was clearly devoted to his soldiers and his mission. His solid leadership showed on all levels. I was treated like a professional. These D Co guys respected what I could do for them. A platoon leader asked me to teach his men a class on basic Arabic. I made up flash cards for them. I made up signs for them to use in crowd-control situations.

This unit was the *only* unit in which I never experienced any discomfort or harassment. No one made inappropriate comments or stepped out of line. Even months later, when I ran into those guys, they always said, "Hey! You were our linguist in Baghdad!" They never said, "Hey! You were that chick we had with us!"—as so many other Army guys did.

I was in Dura, the area on the outskirts of Baghdad where I'd been before. I was out again as a translator with Delta Company, 1/187.

We walked down the street. I talked to families one at a time and asked if anyone had weapons, knew of any caches, or was aware of any terrorists/criminals in the area. The people were friendly and open. They wanted to talk to me. The stories were remarkably consistent—no caches, no terrorists. There were only individual household weapons and several abandoned military pieces in the area, including artillery and an APC (armored personnel carrier).

As we went through the neighborhood, children swarmed around us. They experimented with their few words of English.

"What's your name? What's your name?"

"How are you? How are you?"

"One dollar. One dollar."

They clustered around, and after a time we grew more familiar. There was laughter and giggling. Everyone relaxed.

The last time I was here, I told a few of them my name, and now they chanted it: "Kayla! Kayla! Kayla!"

One boy, a little older, maybe a teenager, asked my name as well. When I told him, he said, "No! You are Britney Spears!" From then on he or his friends called out "Britney! Britney!" I laughed and shook my head. I don't even like Britney Spears, but I knew they meant it as a compliment.

Throughout my deployment I was constantly amazed at how far and fast American pop culture has spread. Even with sanctions in place, Iraqis all knew Britney Spears. And they all knew Michael Jackson and Shakira. (Shakira made sense to me because she's part Lebanese.) But there were also slews of VCDs imported through Asian countries. VCDs are these cheap knock-off DVDs. They have Chinese, Korean, and Arabic subtitles. Some of them are very badly done; taped with handheld video cameras from the screens in movie theaters—you can see the theater's exit signs in the corner. You can see people standing up and walking out. Once we settled in, soldiers bought stacks of these illegal VCDs. I bought *Finding Nemo* and *Dirty Dancing;* I managed to purchase *The Lord of the Rings—The Return of the King* on VCD even before it was available in theaters in the States. After a while, we were routinely picking up VCDs for very little money to play on laptops or portable DVD players. At some later point we also began to buy small Discmans that play VCDs when plugged into cheap televisions we also bought from the locals.

(Later families back home also began to send televisions to their sons and daughters in Iraq. The Army was never able to provide troops with enough air conditioners, so sometime in the summer, when temperatures reached 130 degrees, families began shipping air conditioners to Iraq. There was a story that one mom collected a lot of money and then shipped her son's unit something like a hundred air conditioners she'd bought at Wal-Mart.)

So we got to the end of the street and approached the APC. The families who lived in the nearest compounds came out and gave us dates and bread from woven plates. The food was delicious, a welcome break from MREs. I especially loved the bread—like pita but larger, maybe a foot in diameter, thin and still warm. Around the APC were scattered Iraqi army uniforms. As they deserted the soldiers apparently left even their clothes. I idly wondered if they had civilian clothes with them or if they ran off in their underwear.

We poked around the vehicle, retrieving unspent rounds. I looked through the record book. A few local men talked to the guards we posted. I was called over to translate. They explained how the men in the APC buried their extra ammunition by the side of the road in mounds of dirt. They showed us, and we started to dig. More men and boys joined us. It became a strange scene of soldiers and locals digging up box after box of 50-cal ammunition. Hundreds and hundreds of rounds.

The locals helped us load the ammo onto a bus to transport to the UXO pit where EOD (explosive ordnance disposal) teams would destroy everything. (These explosions, every day or so, were very jarring when unexpected.) The people did not want this stuff in their neighborhood. They worried—with good reason—that their children could get injured.

There were unexploded shells everywhere in this country.

Our shells, their shells—who knew? Bomblets from our cluster bombs were in fields, yards, gardens. When we found them we marked the locations and called EOD to come and destroy them in place. We warned locals to stay away. *Don't touch anything! Keep your children away at all costs!* But children in any country are hard to watch all the time, and forbidden fruit is always the sweetest.

So there was always a concern that some kid would get blown up. But what could we do? There weren't many EOD teams available, and there was a vast quantity of UXO waiting to be destroyed. We did our best but simply couldn't keep up. Several locals pointed out UXO to us, and we marked the areas with white engineer tape and *U-X-O* written on them. I told locals that "special soldiers" (I had no clue how to say EOD in Arabic) would come to take care of it.

They asked, "When?"

I could only say, "Soon, God willing."

There were five artillery pieces in the neighborhood, in addition to the APC and a BM-21 (a Soviet multiple-rocket launcher). We didn't want to leave anything there in usable condition for fear it could be turned against us. The locals didn't want it there anyway. Unfortunately we also didn't have the ability to take it all away with us, so what couldn't be towed had to be destroyed in place.

Dismantling the BM-21 was the coolest. I got to use my Leatherman to cut the wires at the back. This was particularly exciting because I had a pathetic Leatherman. It was very girly—my ex-husband gave it to me, and the gift may have contributed to our divorce. It certainly showed his lack of understanding of my position. I'm in the Army! But he gave me this wine-and-cheese Leatherman. The "Flair" variety. It actually had a shrimp fork, a butter knife, and (more usefully) a bottle opener and a corkscrew. But Army guys all kidded me about it. I called it my "chick Leatherman" or "fag Leatherman." So using it for this cool job of cutting the wires on a BM-21 was very satisfying.

A soldier set a thermite charge on the engine of the APC. It burned right through the engine block and smoldered for hours. They sent another charge down the barrel of one of the artillery pieces.

A few soldiers from the line company decided to shoot two AT-4 (antitank guided) missiles at the rocket launcher. As they set up to fire the missiles, everyone got a thrill. (We didn't do this sort of thing every day.) Eight guys got out cameras to take a picture of the one guy who shot the AT-4. The cameras all snapped at almost the same time. But the missiles did a surprisingly small amount of damage. Inadvertently a patch of underbrush caught fire.

Later that same day, we stopped at a field near the intersection of two highways. We saw kids playing soccer near an abandoned artillery piece. We drove right into the field and got out. We walked around for a few minutes. Then someone saw, or noticed, or realized.

"Oh, shit! This whole fucking field is full of UXO!"

And it was. UXO was everywhere, just littering the ground. And kids were running around. People were flocking to see these fascinating foreigners. The soldiers I was with were convinced that one misstep would blow us all to pieces.

Strangely I wasn't even afraid. It didn't seem like it could be real, exactly, and though I was extremely cautious, I wasn't terrified the way I might have guessed I would be. We all began to step in the footsteps of the person walking in front of us, and continued the mission. We checked the artillery piece, and I sought out the oldest among the locals—a couple of college kids—and explained to them the gravity of the situation.

In Arabic I said: "This place is very dangerous. You must not let children play here."

"Children are impossible to control," they responded. "You can tell them anything, but as soon as you look away, they do it anyway."

"But they could die!" I emphasized. "Explosion! Big danger! Bombs everywhere!"

"Clean it up," they suggested.

I tried to explain, again, about the scarcity of EOD.

A young lieutenant joined me as I attempted to persuade these college students. Again and again we emphasized the danger. We encouraged them to take the children and leave the area. No one moved. They continued to follow us. I could not understand. In America if you tell people they may die if they don't leave, they leave! Don't they? Do I fundamentally misunderstand American culture, or is Iraq just wildly different? After half an hour or more, they finally gathered the children and left.

Very carefully and slowly, we backed our trucks out over the tire tracks we had made on the drive in. On the road again, we breathed easier. We called in the grid coordinate, and waited for a while. Nothing happened. No one came.

I was not entirely sure what was going on but found myself sitting in the back of a Humvee with the very cute lieutenant with an angular nose. We weren't doing anything much, so I struck up a conversation.

I opened with: "So what route did you take to becoming an officer, Sir?"

I tended to ask this question whenever I met an officer, since there are basically three main ways to become one. These are: West Point, Reserve Officers Training Corps (ROTC), and Officer Candidate School (OCS). (For myself I never would have done West Point. It's basic training for four years. Really hardcore— stringent, extreme. It's not my personality. Nor was I the sort of person during college who would have participated in ROTC and then automatically been commissioned as an officer when I graduated. So my route would have been OCS.)

"ROTC," he said.

"So where did you go to college, Sir?"

"Austin. UT Austin."

"I majored in lit at Bowling Green State University in Ohio. What was your major, Sir?"

"History. And political science."

"Oh, really," I said, taking more of an interest. "A history major? Have you read *A People's History of the United States* by Howard Zinn? I really love that book."

The lieutenant smiled. I noticed that his blond hair was quite long for a soldier.

"Oh, you like Zinn, huh? You must read Noam Chomsky, right? And listen to the Dead Kennedys?"

He was teasing me, sure, but if you're a liberal and you do like Howard Zinn, then you probably read Chomsky, too. And you've probably listened to the Dead Kennedys if you're my age and his age. Still, I couldn't believe how he pegged me so quickly. I was intrigued. Even though I knew some bright people in Military Intelligence, I hadn't met an infantry soldier who could chat so casually about Chomsky and Zinn while sitting next to a field full of UXO.

That was how he signaled his own interests and political leanings. A little insider's reference that probably a lot of other people in the military would not necessarily get because most soldiers were not going to have a clue about Howard Zinn. It became this little bond between us.

We talked about his time in Afghanistan as part of Operation Anaconda. I'd heard a lot of scattered references to Anaconda that spring and summer from a number of soldiers, but it was one of those things that was bad enough that no one wanted to talk about it too much. Apparently they experienced a three-day firefight in the mountains. In the snow—with no resupply.

"You know," Lieutenant Samuels said, "I'm thinking that this field is the most UXO I've ever seen in one place. More than I ever saw in one place in Afghanistan, that's for sure."

I knew there were a lot of minefields in Afghanistan. So this impressed me. It also impressed me that he stayed so *calm*.

A few days later there was an urgent call for QRF (quick reaction force).

There's been an explosion.

Soldiers are down. Civilians are hurt. We need to move. *Now*.

We're getting there, and I'm thinking: Wait, wait. Fuck this. I know where we are—

It's the same road as a few days ago, the same streets, the same neighborhood. Only this time we're moving fast, very fast. Everything in overdrive, fast-forward motion. Honking around curves, kids in the streets leaping back and out of the way. People we pass way more subdued, but waving us around the blind curves, telling us it's clear. Like a retake of the same scene, only played for tragedy this time. I can feel myself tensing up.

Once there, I recognize it all. We were here. We marked the door to that compound with white engineer tape. *U-X-O.* The locals would not have any idea what these English letters meant, but the intention was to warn other soldiers who might be doing patrols. And to mark it for EOD. We don't bother to mark the UXOs in Arabic because it's usually the locals who call the unexploded mines to our attention.

We get out of the Humvees, and things are bad. The explosion was in a compound, but nothing else about the circumstances is immediately clear.

We find three locals on the ground, bleeding, already getting treated by other soldiers. Our wounded guys are being transported out in the backs of Humvees. Not so lucky are these locals, their bleeding stanched by field dressings, their legs already caked in dried blood. But everyone is doing their job— pulling guard or treating the injured. Focused.

My job: translate. But what and to whom? Everyone ignoring me. It's not a situation for which I have trained.

What can I do? How can I help?

A young local in a blue shirt, sweating, his hair slicked back as if for a prom. His English is clear enough.

"You need help."

It's a question, I know, but I take it wrong for a moment. He wants to help *me.*

"You speak English? Stay here and help. Yes," I say. "Thank you."

I ask the soldier in charge how I can help.

"Grab my Kevlar and weapon from over there," he points at

the ground a couple of meters away. He shouts at other soldiers in the vicinity. "Maintain your guard positions!"

I grab his stuff and hand it over. He puts on his Kevlar.

"What do you need?" I ask. "How can I help? I'm a translator."

"Tape. I can't find my tape." He's treating a local who is less seriously wounded. "In my CLS bag."

I look in his CLS (combat lifesaver) bag but I can't find tape. I notice the Delta Company first sergeant pulling away in a Humvee.

"First Sergeant, we need *tape*." I'm out of breath, no doubt looking a little wired. "Do you have your CLS bag?"

No. But he does have a big civilian first-aid kit, and that's probably better. He hands it to me. And he's gone. Not a word passes his lips.

I'm back at the scene again. Deliver the tape. Gloves on. Conscientious. Still feeling okay, despite all the blood. The mood remains tense. One guy on the ground—it's obvious—worse off than the others. The medic—that's who's been directing every-one—is starting an IV on the man he's treating. The man is rel-atively calm. I reassure him in Arabic as best I can and then move over to the other small group.

"Can someone please tell this guy to hold still?!"

A seriously wounded man is thrashing.

I step forward. Kneel. In Arabic I repeat the instructions. Over and over. "Stay still. Don't move. Please." The badly wounded man calls out to God. Moans. Writhes.

The two soldiers treating him have field dressings in place to stop the bleeding. They are attempting to start an IV to replace lost fluids.

I move in closer.

I beg him, "*Ya hajji, la t'hark.* Don't move." I try to explain.

In Arabic: "We're trying to help you. This will hurt a bit, but it's to help you."

Panicked, he looks through me, if he looks at me at all.

I ask the kid in the blue shirt to help me calm him. He tries. I get more supplies—a tube, another needle. But the soldiers can't find a vein. The dying man's veins are collapsing as he goes deeper and deeper into shock.

I'm in close now, so close I'm holding the badly hurt guy's legs, covered in drying blood. Holding the legs still until they can get an IV going.

It's not working. There are problems here. The man starts to scream again. I'm concentrating on helping this man, but we are not finding a vein. I'm holding his legs, holding them still. Hoping this is going to work.

The soldiers yell for the medic, but he calls back over that he can't or won't leave the guy he's treating.

"Just do what you can! Do what you are trained to do!"

I'm amazed at his focus.

My breathing is getting faster and faster, and one of the soldiers stares at me. I consciously slow my breathing.

They bring over the third wounded local, his leg broken in two places. I check on him.

I move between the three injured men. The first is doing pretty well. The young man in the blue shirt is holding an IV bag up for him. I kneel to reassure him that more help is coming. His pants are cut off, his dick and balls are there, and there's blood. Flies hovering everywhere, everywhere. No fucking respect for the crisis at hand, I think, even as I realize that this is illogical. Flies are flies. I brush them off the bleeding cut on his head.

When he realizes he is naked from the waist down, he feebly moves to pull his shirt to cover himself. I recognize the motion, and try to reassure him.

"My brother, that isn't important. Just hold on. An ambulance is coming. We're taking you to a hospital."

Periodically the medic yells: "Where the fuck is the FLA [ambulance]?"

More soldiers arrive. More medics. A medic orders the kid in the blue shirt to leave.

"Let him stay!" I'm yelling. "He's helping. He speaks good English. He's helping me!"

Among the new arrivals is a lieutenant colonel. He wants me to interrogate these wounded men.

"Ask him," the colonel is shouting at me. "Ask him why the fuck these ragheads took our guys to this compound *knowing* there was a UXO in it."

"Because of the UXO," I try to explain.

"Because of the UXO? They were trying to kill our guys?! Ask him!"

I look up, but I can't bring myself to speak. Why did the locals lead our guys to the UXO? I think. Like these guys *wanted* to hurt us? And now one of *them* is *dying*?

"You stupid asshole," I say, but my voice is only in my head. "They're scared for their kids." Out loud I mutter: "I am not interrogating the guy that's dying."

But the colonel's gone off. No one responds to what I say.

I hear an officer: "Fuck these motherfuckers. One of *them* set it off."

The colonel sees me again.

"Go tell those people not to go in there." He points at a

crowd gathered two hundred meters away by an intersection, kept back by the guards.

"We did that, Sir," I say as calmly as I can. "We did that. A couple of days ago. I'll mark the doors again—in Arabic this time. Maybe that will help."

He looks hard at me.

"Soldier," the colonel says. "Just do what I am telling you to do. Right *now*."

Lieutenant Samuels, the guy I met from a few nights ago who reads Zinn and Chomsky, is here too, and he sees I'm getting ready to fight. He sees that I am not noticing rank. That I just want to do what's right—even if it means yelling at some asshole colonel.

The lieutenant pulls me away.

"Leave it," he says in my ear. "Take a moment. Step *back*."

Hearing this, I do head down the street toward the crowd. And I explain again to the locals that no one should go in there. Avoid UXO. And so forth. Behind me I can *feel* the man dying, and I cannot fucking believe I'm here doing this—instead of helping him.

A local is right in my face.

"We told you about this bomb a couple of days ago." He is so close, I take a step back just to breathe. "Why didn't you fix it? Before it was too late? Now people are hurt."

Almost dead.

"Their family—" And he points. I don't want to look. But I do. A couple of men over there. Brothers, I am told. Women are crying.

I'm trying to explain. "It *was* marked. There is so much UXO. So few soldiers who can remove it. We're trying. We're *trying*."

We get permission for the brothers to come back with us. I gesture to them, and we walk back to the dying man. They see the dying man puke as a soldier gives him mouth-to-mouth. I'm shocked in a numb way that he isn't already dead.

I think: I've been pretty calm, I'm handling this well.

Someone hands me a bottle of water. I don't drink it—just use it to wash off some gore. The brothers talk. They want me to go back down the road. Some more family members have gathered. If the man is going to be moved to a military hospital, I explain, only immediate family can escort him. I go back down the road with them, and there are two wives. They want to come, and then they change their minds.

Moving back again, I see that finally it's time to move the injured men into an ambulance and take them back to the aid station, and take the brothers in a Humvee.

The man who was dying has now been covered with a poncho.

The medic tells me what to say to the other injured men. To keep them calm.

"Say he's only injured. He's very cold. He needs covering."

I repeat these lies.

In a Humvee we drive back to the "hospital," that is, the aid station in our compound. I sit in the backseat and I get to be still for a moment.

I just want to cry, but I don't. I can't. I have to be hard, strong, in front of these soldiers, these *guys*. I blink the tears back and breathe deeply.

I'm wondering: Why the fuck did soldiers go in there after we fucking *marked* it? That makes no sense. And the locals all saying it was a *soldier* who set it off.

Once we arrive, I get out of the Humvee. In what I think is

the smartest thing I've done all day, I reach out for support. I get help, sending someone to fetch another Arabic linguist I know, a friend of mine in Human Intelligence (HUMINT), to translate for one of the injured men while the doctors treat him. The main crisis feels over. Easing. Slowing.

I help as they treat the guy with the broken leg. His name is Mahmoud. He has three sons and a daughter. He gets morphine, finally, for the pain.

I go to talk to the relatives of the dead man. They tell me his name is Ali and that he has a son and a daughter.

His brothers ask, "What will the Army do for our family?"

Under Islamic law, there is a thing called *di'ah*. If you accidentally cause someone's death, you pay their family. It is your debt.

"We're the American Army, and we don't do that," I explain.

I feel terrible. I wish there is something I could do. I wish there was some way I could pay them myself.

Sergeant Quinn finds me and offers me Gatorade. He knows what has been going on, and he is more compassionate and gentle with me than I have ever seen him. I realize, drinking the Gatorade, that I haven't had anything to eat or drink in hours and hours. It has gotten dark. I feel, suddenly, shaken and drained.

Finally I am no longer needed. The injured men are being transported to a real hospital. I go back to our site. Staff Sergeant Moss tells me to take the night off, but she doesn't speak to me otherwise. I need to talk to someone—this is probably the only time I could have reached out to SSG Moss, but she acts disinterested. I tell Lauren the whole story, and I finally cry. She sympathizes and comforts me for a moment. I can't possibly sleep yet—still wired, full of nervous energy. Strangely I realize that all I want, the only thing I really want, is to be told that I did a good job out there today.

With a start I remember that I never asked if all of our guys are okay. I walk back to the aid station to ask a medic. He reassures me that they will all live.

At the aid station there is a chaplain. He sees me and walks over to talk. He tells me he was out there today. That he saw me. Watched me.

"You did a good job," he says. "You really comforted those men. It must have been hard on you—it was hard on me, and I was just watching. But you did a really great job."

I never have had much use for chaplains, but this man, Captain Bridges, somehow says exactly what I need to hear. I am reassured, calmed.

I go talk to my HUMINT friend who speaks Arabic. He tells me that they refused to allow the dead man to be transported back to his family in an FLA. This makes some sense, since an ambulance might be needed if more soldiers get injured tonight.

But then he tells me that they decided to transport the dead man in the back of a commandeered pickup truck.

I'm taken aback by this.

"Damn," I say, feeling tears again. "That feels real disrespectful. Don't you think?"

"Listen," he says. "It's way better than their first idea. They were debating whether or not just to strap the body to the hood of a Humvee."

NORTH

Suddenly and unexpectedly our team got pulled out of Baghdad, yanked back to D-Main to sit on our collective asses for several days. Given the supreme need 1/187 had for translators, and given a powerful lack of available Arabic linguists, this made no sense to me. Then we were moved south to join 1st Brigade (BDE), where we did nothing for a couple more days. Now at last we joined a convoy heading north toward Mosul. This was all frustrating beyond belief. The only constant in our lives was movement. Pulled here and there.

By this time, our shirts and DCUs (desert camouflage uniforms) were utterly filthy and salt stained. We just sat and sweated. When we entered Iraq we'd worn the JSLIST suits to protect us from biological and chemical attack. When we were finally allowed to take off these suits after three weeks or so, we switched to our second pair of DCUs and wore those until they stood up on their own. Then we put back on the DCUs we'd worn before we were in-country—uniforms we'd considered dirty before but that now appeared clean by comparison. Occasionally, a couple of times in Baghdad, we did do some hand-washing of clothes, but nothing ever felt clean.

The convoy commander was a prick.

"Today's drive will last between five and seven hours," he announced. "Three hundred kilometers straight from here to Qayyarah West Airfield. Q-West will be the main headquarters of 1st Brigade, and it is currently in poor shape. Dirt piles, cratered airstrips, broken concrete. You get the general idea." He paused. "Oh, one more thing. We're in a hurry today. There will be no stops. No breaks. Once we move, we keep moving. If you need to piss, piss in a bottle."

And with these words, off we went. I drove our truck, and I was thinking how this captain had given no consideration to the girls on his GAC. Had anyone informed him that peeing in a bottle for a girl was not the same as it was for a guy? Guys could pee out the damned door! (They didn't—but they could.) Nor had this guy considered how difficult it was for a girl to piss in a bottle while driving a Humvee. But "no stops, no breaks" meant "no stops, no breaks." So we started rolling and we kept rolling.

The scenery distracted us from yet another boring drive, at least for a while. There was a gentle transition from desert to rolling grassy hills as we moved north through Samarra and Tikrit. We saw scenic mountains in the distance, and men or boys herd fat fluffy sheep with a donkey or a dog in tow. We saw women in *hijabs,* and when they spotted us female soldiers, they smiled shy smiles. They waved, and we waved back. We saw brightly colored clothing flutter on clotheslines outside uniformly grayish brown houses. Children cheered us, though they were just as likely to beg for food or water by using the universal symbol: repeatedly raising their hands to their mouths. We passed open-air markets or city shops with stands piled high with vegetables and fruits. Despite the war, daily life continued. Roses in so many yards, flowers in so many gardens. Beauty carefully cultivated even amid such poverty and oppression.

North. The mood changed after a time. We slowly drove past 4th Infantry Division (4 ID) guys looking mean and ugly. They stood on top of their trucks, their weapons pointed directly at civilians. The civilians were moving tensely through ordinary activities. Acting as if there were no damned guns aimed at their heads—and these were women with children in tow! What could these locals possibly have done? Why was this intimidation necessary? No one explained anything, but it looked weird and felt wrong.

The drive was beyond dull after a while, and I was left to reflections. In Baghdad with D Co, the primary effort had been to build a bond with the locals, carefully nurturing relationships and building *trust*. We got to a point where locals in certain neighborhoods knew us, and knew they could trust us. Maybe because those guys had already been in "the Ghan," or maybe due to better leadership, they grasped the high stakes. They acted like the U.S. Army, not bulldozing in a minute what it takes months to build up.

In the last several days I'd heard all sorts of horror stories: soldiers busting down civilians' doors and dragging people into the streets; soldiers purchasing a damned sheep only to muzzle it and then beat it to death. Soldiers taking shots at people as they ran away, or shooting up entire cars of people as they approached a manned checkpoint (women, children, whatever) because they didn't stop in time.

We all knew that local women were afraid of soldiers and would not necessarily stop at checkpoints. They were not used to dealing with men, let alone American men. They would see

American men with guns and panic. If an American sees a checkpoint with armed soldiers, the American stops. Wouldn't she? But in Iraq there was a lot of confusion. From what I heard, things got out of hand pretty often.

Fucking mayhem was what it was. And meanwhile there were *no signs* in Arabic to alert locals that they were approaching a checkpoint. No respect for the customs of the people, for the rhythms of their lives, for the shit they've had to suffer. There was way too little attempt to communicate with the people. Too many soldiers acting like it was *shoot-em-up* time. I already missed 3rd Brigade. None of them ever said they wanted to feel what it might be like to shoot someone. Or thought killing a local might be cool. These 1st Brigade soldiers made me uncomfortable.

Soon, however, reflections were overwhelmed by a serious need to pee. It had to be psychological—the damned speech. If the convoy commander hadn't said we couldn't, who knows? But now after a few hours bouncing in the backseat, Lauren can't take it any longer.

"I really have to pee," she said. "I can't hold it. I'm really gonna have to piss. I cannot wait. I'm gonna have to do it right here."

We all laughed as Lauren started to curse the convoy commander for forcing this indignity upon her. Cursing herself for downing a big milkshake mixed with coffee right before we left. Quickly Lauren sliced off the top of a water bottle with a knife, dropped her pants, and pissed. A clean move. And then she hurled the whole mess out the window.

Five minutes after the cup spattered in the dirt, a truck up ahead broke and died. The convoy cruised to a halt for repairs.

And in the meantime dozens of grateful soldiers rushed to relieve themselves. Lauren could not believe her lousy luck. The guys in the truck behind us announced how impressed they were with her acrobatic feat.

I was spared a lesson in how to pee while driving. But I heard later some other girls do accomplish this maneuver. I didn't ask for details. It just did not qualify as something I really wanted to know.

We got to Q-West in the evening.

Soon afterward this random 1st BDE infantry guy sauntered over.

"Hey. You MI?"

"That's right."

"Welcome." He was like eighteen, nineteen. "Seen any combat yet?"

"A little." No one eager to talk. No one in the mood at the moment to humor this.

"Yeah," the guy said, puffing himself up and stretching his arms. A little yawn. Casual-like. "I got a kill just last week. Man, I gotta tell you. It was the *coolest*. To see what happens when this dude got it. I can't even begin to explain." He looked at us to see how we were doing.

Not one of us said a thing. Don't try, I'm thinking.

"I warned the dude," he continued. "I was yelling at him, 'Stop, motherfucker.' But he kept coming. He kept coming."

"Listen—" I began to say. I didn't want to get involved, but I didn't want to hear this.

"Man, it was so *cool*," the kid repeated. Cleared his throat. He sounded scratchy all of a sudden. Like the kid he really was.

Swapped tones on us, going from hard-core to altogether less macho.

"But it's my job and all, y'know?" he said, a little shaky. "I got a job to do. That's why I'm here. To get a job done. Y'know?"

After a moment he wandered off. Like that's what he came to say, and now it was done.

No one spoke. We moved into the night like it was a bad dream, which—in a way—it was.

I mean: What *do* you say?

Real packages arrived for the first time. Since we'd been kept moving, attached to one unit and then another and another, we'd been a hard team to find. Mail never seemed to get to us on time. And now boxes and boxes of stuff all at once for everyone. After so many weeks of nothing, this was amazing. *Real* packages with stuff in them. I got envelopes and treats. Potato chips. Cheese and crackers. Granola bars and Special K cereal bars. Sucky chewies. Pogey bait. Lauren got cigarettes, romance novels, and magazines. And she got some fine-smelling lotion, which was a very big deal for us.

Maybe because the war was pretty much over and all, or officially *announced* as almost over, the packages raised hopes that this signaled the beginning of the end of our time there. Everyone ready to go home. Rumors almost every day. Talk about a midsummer return or, if not, then certainly by Labor Day. Already folks were planning what they'd do when they got back. It all felt unreal to me, but there was no reason to doubt it *could* happen.

This day the packages arrived may not have made it Disney World, but it certainly felt like Christmas.

——

Lauren had a wisdom tooth out, which left her high on painkillers. Acting silly. Giggling all the time. So we chilled out near our position, reading our books and magazines, eating a little candy, and trying to stay in the shade, where it was a little cooler. The heat was brutal.

I vaguely registered some infantry guys walking over to drop trash in a burn pit about ten meters off. They lit it, and then they were gone.

A putrid smell of smoke, but that was not new. Still, after a few more moments it got our attention. We heard a strange crackling sound. Lauren looked up. "Fire!" she yelled. The dry grass around the burn pit had leaped into flames.

The fire was spreading with terrible speed and, with a breeze blowing, our truck with our stuff was going to get hit soon.

"What the hell? I thought those guys—"

"Incompetent bastards," Lauren said, still hazy.

The guys lit the fire not thinking it might jump out of the pit, and didn't bother to monitor it properly to make sure it didn't.

But it did. And here we were in the middle of it with no one around to help us put it out.

Fire moves fast over ground when it hasn't rained in weeks.

We ran. Right into the burning grass. We stomped and stomped, a crazy dance with our boots hitting the flames. We grabbed our e-tools (small folding shovels) and used them to beat the flames. The ground was too tight and dry to scoop handfuls of dirt to throw, so it was the rain dance we did. But we were losing the fight. The fire kept moving outward in every direction.

Quinn arrived to help us, but where was Staff Sergeant Moss? Who knew? She was always somewhere else when shit happened.

After a time some infantry guys—*not* the guys who set it—saw us out there dancing in the flames, and they joined us. It got scary, but the number of soldiers stamping made a difference. We halted the fire's progress and then got it under control.

So that was the scene. A bunch of soldiers putting out a grass fire. But before we stopped it, it burned a hundred square feet.

Man, were we *pissed.*

We got even angrier when one guy called out to everyone, "Great job, gentlemen!"

Hey, we're not all gentlemen! Lauren and I worked our asses off. We were first on the scene. But none of that seemed to matter at all.

Sergeant Quinn wanted to talk to someone from the unit that started the fire. So we kept our eyes on their bunker. Before too long a guy stepped out to smoke a cigarette.

"*Hey, you!*" Lauren yelled. "Yes, *you.* Get over here."

Now Lauren was this little person, as I've said, and she looked so sweet. But that was misleading. However, it was never a good idea to shout at a soldier when you didn't know him. Or know his rank. Like, for instance, as this soldier approached, we saw he was a first sergeant.

"What's the problem here?" he asked.

"Your damned men almost *torched* our position. They lit a burn pit and they didn't mind it and—"

He looked like we did have a problem, but it wasn't the problem we were talking about.

"Listen," he said angrily to Lauren. "Let me offer you some advice. Don't *ever* tell any of my men what to do. And don't bother me again."

He lumbered away.

———

The next day we got moved out beyond the perimeter to set up a listening post (LP) on a nearby mountain. All the buildings here were empty shells—walls with no doors, no windows, no ceilings. Lauren and I claimed a room, rigged a "roof" of ponchos for shade, and set up our cots. A degree of privacy for the first time since we'd been in-country. Resting in there when we were not on shift, we'd talk. Open up to each other more. I was finally beginning to feel like I had someone around I could trust.

It didn't last. After a couple of days, our team fell apart. Lauren's wisdom tooth wound had gotten infected, so she went back to Q-West to have a dentist look at it. Leaving behind her gear and personal stuff, she figured it was minor and she'd be back, maybe the same day.

But she didn't come back that day.

And then that same night SSG Moss got dysentery. It came with the country; everyone got sick at some point. Vomiting. Diarrhea. Everything running out of her at both ends, and it might have been funny if it hadn't been awful. A plastic bag attached to her ass, and another plastic bag for her mouth. She looked so pathetic and smelled so bad I began to feel sorry for her. Couldn't help it. I didn't want or need this. I didn't want her *useless*. This was bad for all of us, especially with Lauren gone.

So we were down from four to two. With running ops around the clock, and pulling security, this meant Quinn and I would be awake all night.

Now Sergeant Quinn was a guy I didn't much like at first. Stiff and official. Needed to prove he was right about everything. Made certain he always got the last word. He'd read a lot, knew a ton, but there was this need to let everyone know what he knew.

And basically leaving me feeling irritable around him much of the time. Testy and *tested*.

To cope with the inevitable, we fixed a huge amount of instant coffee mixed with cocoa powder and lukewarm water. A potent mix. Around 9 P.M. we began our dosage, and managed to finish our entire bottles by midnight.

The LP was a few kilometers off from Q-West on a hilly bedrock, elevated but remote. The air cooled down at night, and the softly swaying sound of the wind had a lulling effect. By this point, SSG Moss had passed out, her groans dissipated down to an open-mouth breathing we couldn't hear from where we were in the truck.

SGT Quinn started to twitch, but once he did, it wasn't long before I did, too. The cocoa and coffee having more of an effect than we bargained for.

"Listen," he said, but I couldn't tell if he meant *Listen, I hear something out there* or *Listen, I've got something to say.*

Playing it safe, I listened for both possibilities.

"Do you hear that?" I asked.

At 0215 hours there was a hissing sound somewhere, or I thought there was. Didn't I?

"Do I hear that?" Quinn asked, but I couldn't see his face. Was he mocking me?

"Listen," I said. "Do you see that?"

There was a shadow. Or maybe I just imagined I saw it. A slim crescent moon rose over the horizon, so darkness still prevailed.

"I don't mean to frighten you," Quinn said, frightening me.

"But?"

"But I was wondering—" He stopped for a full minute, and there was only silence. "I was reading about space aliens in this science journal. Something real, I mean. A real science journal. And studies show how likely it is. Likely that they exist, I mean. Space aliens."

"You're messing with me," I said, feeling messed with.

"No. I'm not," Quinn said. "Listen, it's probably bullshit. But I thought I saw—"

"That flashing light a few minutes ago?"

"You saw it, too?"

"What could it be?"

"Now you're messing with *me*."

Silence.

We talked about the movie *Signs* while listening to static on the radio. We got progressively more freaked out. It was absurd; we knew it was comic, laughed about it, but still were getting more nervous and jittery anyway.

"Any more coffee?" Quinn asked.

"I think we've had enough."

The night went like that. An early Halloween this year. Panic-inducing phantoms and crazy chatter about space aliens.

By the time the sun came up, we'd thoroughly freaked each other out.

But I really felt okay about Quinn after that. He's really all right, I decided.

We never told anyone about our paranoid night together tripping on coffee and cocoa, more spooked by aliens than a very real human enemy.

Lauren never came back. While she was at Q-West for her infection, she got word that her husband had gotten dangerously ill, something no one could say for sure what it was, and that she would be going home as well. It all happened so fast, she never had a chance to get back in touch with us. Left everything behind, and I was left to inventory her stuff.

After a few more days at our hillside LP, we also returned to Q-West. As barren and austere as it is, Q-West still felt like civilization after several days in the wilderness.

Pretty randomly I bumped into the first sergeant Lauren and I had yelled at. The one whose men had lit the fire that almost burned down our position.

"Where's the sparkplug?" he asked, holding a package.

"Who?"

"That tiny female who yelled at me. Don't say you don't know who she is."

"Yeah," I said. "I know her. But she's gone. Her husband is very sick, and she got sent home."

"Tough break," he said, sounding like he meant it. "Listen. This was for her, but maybe you could tell her I tried to get it to her. Or maybe you can all have it."

He handed me a package.

"Just some stuff we got together, the guys and me," he said. "A peace offering . . ."

I opened the box, and it was soap, toothpaste, chocolates, pretzels, Cheez Doodles, a *Maxim* magazine or two, and some cocoa mix.

"Hey, you don't have to—"

"Hey, take it. Our way to square this one away, okay?"

A good leader, I'm thinking. A good man. I'm already wanting to tell Lauren about it.

I missed her already.

MOUNTAIN TIME

"So what's this now again?" Quinn asks.

"It's the Femmes. The Violent Femmes."

"It's—cool. I like it, I think." He begins to remove the earphones.

"That's good, Geoff. But give it more time. Keep listening."

He's so tense looking. Stoic. It's odd to watch him. But also fascinating.

After a minute more, I wonder. He's sitting there motionless, like he's frozen solid. Has my MP3 player died? Is he faking me out?

He's looking so damned puzzled, it's almost sweet.

"Maybe we should try something else," he says.

"No, no," I demur. "Don't stop, Geoff. Give it a minute. Remember this is supposed to be a *lesson*."

"Maybe something else, though. What else you got?" Trying to act relaxed. Failing.

"Well," I consider, holding up the player for a look. "Let's think."

It's my music appreciation class for Geoff, and I'm giving it my best. He's a tough sell. Since the night at the LP when we shared that special moment freaked out together, I've relaxed around him. He still annoys me sometimes with his "I'm so smart" attitude, but I try to develop a little more compassion. Not judge so hard. And as I lighten up, he starts to share accounts of his very sheltered childhood in Ohio. We're both from Ohio; you'd think this means we have things in common. Not too likely. Here's a guy whose mother considered *The Simpsons* a bad influence. So she told Geoff not to watch *The Simpsons*. Okay. I know parents can be bizarre. That's not what gets me. The crazy thing is: Geoff has never seen *The Simpsons*. He grasps some rudimentary concepts about Homer and Bart. He knows it's a cartoon— but that's it. His mom says *no,* and Geoff says, *Okay, Mom.*

What twenty-one-year-old guy in his right mind avoids a cartoon show because his mother says he should?

We're into May, and Quinn and I have been stuck on the same team for months. Dealt with Staff Sergeant Moss and everything else. Got separated for a week or so in Baghdad when I was tasked out with D Co, but otherwise we've been together from day one. Honestly, I had zero tolerance for the guy at first.

So he's inexperienced and inept in all sorts of ways. Focused on narrow details he can get right, and understands thoroughly. But would not run from his cage even if someone left the door wide open. I almost pity him sometimes. Then sometimes he's just a jackass, and I feel he deserves what he gets. But after we stay up all night imagining spaceships and aliens, I work on seeing his potential. The inner Geoff. I gently try to encourage this guy to evolve in a more positive direction.

That means music appreciation class. Anyway, it's a start.

On the player I program tunes randomly. Let's give anything else a try. See what comes. I lean back in my seat to watch.

He actually likes some of it, he says. I then try to play my more "accessible" music, nothing too "out there." I'm glad he's giving it a shot.

We talk more now, too. I'm feeling pretty whiny and full of self-pity.

So I'm telling Quinn: "I am never going to find somebody to spend his life with me. People don't like me. Sooner or later everybody leaves me. Even my damn parents never cared for me. No man is ever going to marry me. I am terrible at relationships. My relationships always fail. So I have to face the truth that I am going to be single forever. I am really such a failure."

I'm feeling quite dramatic. Like a martyr doomed to a life without lasting love.

"And I hate it," I continue. "It frustrates me that those things that I consider my best qualities are the same exact things that everyone hates about me. Like the fact that I'm driven. Like the fact that I'm extremely organized. That I'm always pushing myself to learn better and do better and be better. And be more successful. And grow. I think that those are my very best qualities—the most admirable things about me. And almost all the men I've dated end up asking me 'So when are you just going to be happy with the ways things are? Why can't you just accept things? Why don't you just be happy with what you have? Why do you have to be like this?' So these guys always cut me down. Nitpick."

Quinn adjusts his glasses.

"You, you're a nice girl," he says. "You're a good person. You're really okay. You're smart. You're funny. You'll find the right person someday. Someday you'll find that special someone."

Quinn goes on.

"How do you think I feel? The things I believe are the most important things in life are to have a relationship and get married and have children. Or even just have a relationship. But this is something I have never done. Never. So how do you think I feel?"

That stops me. That makes me think.

I am thinking: This fucking guy who has not even *kissed* a girl! He's never found a girl who's even close to being "that special someone," while I've had how many failed relationships? And now he's telling me to hold on to hope?

Still, it's really sweet. Quinn telling me not to lose hope. It touches me. In an odd way his belief that I can find happiness does help me feel hopeful.

We get moved back temporarily to D-Main, where I'm called to appear before a promotion board, my first step toward becoming a noncommissioned officer. As my time in the military passed the three-year mark, it was time for me to become a sergeant. Meaning better pay, for one thing. Also greater responsibilities and authority. I got the maximum score on the board and was proud of myself—it was a tense experience for me, like it was for most people.

But then it looked like the Army screwed up my paperwork. It became anyone's guess how long this was going to take to straighten out.

We moved again to 3rd Brigade, where Staff Sergeant Gardner replaced SSG Moss. One Arabic linguist replacing another. Meanwhile Specialist Reid replaced Lauren. One Korean linguist replacing another.

So we've got Lawyer now, and that's cool. Reid never acted

LOVE MY RIFLE MORE THAN YOU

like he was better than anyone because he went to college or law school. None of that. He never talked down to infantry or other MI.

Gardner replacing Moss at first seemed good, because he could talk about ideas and books. And he listened to a lot of the same music as me, and liked some of the same strange movies I liked.

Staff Sergeant Gardner was a very tall half-Korean in his mid-thirties, a military brat whose dad had also been Army. Gardner was a military man through and through. His wife was also a staff sergeant and an Arabic linguist. We quickly realized that Gardner's career was definitely fast track. And then we realized how pedantic he could be. If I talked to Gardner about practically anything, I was going to get lectured on how much he knew about the topic.

He would lecture me about literature. Which pissed me off— that was my major, after all. Eventually we had a conversation about politics, and it turned out he was this hard-core Republican. Very conservative. I'd cite statistics or facts about social conditions or political issues, and Staff Sergeant Gardner's response would always be the same.

"Can you prove that fact, Williams? I don't know how you can expect me to take that statistic seriously unless you're prepared to back it up with evidence."

And my answer was always the same, though I never said it exactly like this:

"I'm in fucking Iraq, Sergeant Gardner. I do not happen to have a goddamn encyclopedia in my fucking pocket. No, I can't prove it!"

Gardner inevitably said: "Well, I don't believe you."

Still, Staff Sergeant Gardner was a huge improvement over Staff Sergeant Moss. So the guy talked down to us. Big deal. He never almost got me killed.

We pulled mission in the Sinjar Mountains on the Syrian border, colocated with a Pathfinder unit in a small compound.

In other situations Pathfinders established drop zones and landing zones (DZ/LZ) for the parachuting of personnel and equipment. Here they were monitoring the border. Watching for suspicious persons coming across.

The Pathfinders kept to themselves while we were there. They worked with a few Peshmergas—guerrillas fighting for a free Kurdish state. The Peshmerga guys were friendly, but most of them spoke only Kurdish—and I sure didn't. Otherwise our compound was off-limits to locals, so it stayed secluded and *very* quiet.

The physical surroundings there were really quite beautiful. Fantastic vistas and incredible flowers. You could see the whole slope of the mountainside down to the patchwork plains below. You could see for miles. The plants inside the compound were amazingly varied. Pink flowers and purple flowers and pale green flowers that looked like little wontons, as well as bright red poppies that stood out from a considerable distance. There were also flowers I called the evil death bushes because they had really sharp thorns on them. Whenever I got up in the middle of the night to pee, I inevitably stumbled into one of these bushes and scratched my legs.

But there was nothing much to do off shift. Surrounded by hills and open space where we couldn't wander (for security reasons), it got a little tiresome.

The Peshmerga guys provided some minor distraction once in a while.

Once I got woken in the middle of the night because one of the Peshmergas was sick. He needed to speak to the medic who only spoke English. One of the other Peshmerga guys spoke some Arabic. So the sick guy would talk in Kurdish to the other guy who translated into Arabic for me, and I would translate into English to tell the medic. Then the medic would ask a question back, and we'd go to Arabic and then back to Kurdish. And back and forth. It took forever. After we finally gave the sick guy some medicine, suddenly all these Peshmerga guys appeared and lined up with ailments. They all wanted to tell us about their medical problems.

"I have a toothache."

"My stomach hurts."

Several of them pulled up pants legs or shirtfronts.

"Would you please ask the doctor to have a look at this scar for me? I got this in the Iran-Iraq war." (I don't know why, but Iraqis *loved* to show you their scars.)

And I was stunned. "What do you expect us to do?"

The Kurdish locals also played a game we called "rock," though this was certainly not its real name. It was a little like checkers. They would draw a grid on the ground and have sides with light rocks or dark rocks. Despite the immense language barrier, the Pathfinders learned to communicate. They learned how to play rock, for instance. Some of the Pathfinders got pretty good at it, too, and would win once in a while against the Peshmergas.

Occasionally the Peshmergas would cook for us. Though all I ever saw them prepare for themselves was a big vat of rice with chickpeas. No spices. Nothing. And that was truly all I *ever* saw them eat.

But mainly there was way too much time to think.

My own warped past came back to me as raw material for unpleasant thoughts and loopy dreams spinning through my brain: messy relationships with boys that in retrospect appeared utterly ridiculous. My lousy marriage. (What *was* I thinking?) My dad, too, who I heard from my stepmom was having a hard time with my deployment. Especially as we moved past the tenth anniversary of my sister's death, I worried about him. Might I be getting a Red Cross message soon—the way Lauren did? (Not to be morbid.)

Before things got too gloomy, we got pulled again. Within a week we went back down to the plains to Tal Afar, a desert airfield about thirty miles from the Syrian border and thirty miles west of Mosul, where we reunited with our platoon. The mountains weren't cool, exactly, but coming back to the desert you realized it was twenty degrees hotter down there. It could reach close to 130 Fahrenheit at the airfield. It was only May, and the heat was miserable. Day or night, you never stopped sweating. I'd walk to the shower tent and get clean and put on clean clothes. I'd walk back outside and within five minutes I sweated through everything again. As clothes dried they looked tie-dyed because the salt left a white residue. (You could see the outline of girls' bras this way.)

Eventually the airfield got swamp coolers for the thirty-man tents. You filled the swamp cooler with water, and it blew humid air into the tent. It might cool off the area in the immediate vicinity a dozen degrees or so, but from a temperature of 130 that's not a great help. That was as close to air-conditioning as they ever had in the tents.

———

I was not finding it easy to be around my own platoon. Guys in my platoon I drank and partied with back in the United States, but here it was not so easy to feel a connection. These guys were not even saying hello to me. They wouldn't even look at me. But they greeted the men on my team.

"Hey, Sergeant Gardner. Hey, Sergeant Quinn. Hey, Reid. Long time. How you been?"

I was getting shunned. The cold shoulder from guys I used to hang with all the time. I had no fucking idea why. No one was talking. No one was telling me anything.

Within a day we were sent back out on mission. I was just as happy to leave, and it wasn't just the heat.

Staff Sergeant Gardner stayed at base to discuss his reenlistment options. So it was only Sergeant Quinn and Specialist Reid and me out in the truck. Our mission was to colocate with a COLT team (combat observation and lasing team) that had an observation post on Sinjar Mountain.

The guys on a COLT team, I learned, were chosen from the best of their MOS, which is 13-Foxtrot, the fire support team or FISTers—an acronym they love. It's a competitive process to be selected for a COLT team. (So all COLT are FISTers, but not all FISTers are COLT.) The FISTers we were to meet were serving as forward observers to watch the Syrian border and call for artillery fire if necessary.

We took the road out of Tal Afar straight west. Everything was fine. We got to the end of the road—literally—and radioed the FISTers, who directed us more or less straight up a mountain.

Okay. Visualize this. It was *very* rocky terrain. Nothing but rocks. No road, no path, no trees or brush. Just rocks. The only differential was rock size. You've got really big rocks, the kind we might call boulders. And you've got smaller rocks, big enough to stop most civilian vehicles in their tracks. And I was driving.

Humvees are remarkable machines. They work almost everywhere and can do almost anything an off-road vehicle needs to do. But this mountain was rocky and it was steep. Very steep. We were going slow, maybe five to ten kilometers an hour, and I was creeping us up, holding tight to the wheel.

Then we slipped a little sideways.

"Hey," Quinn said, popping the passenger door. "Let me ground-guide you."

A sensible call. The goal here was to help avoid the larger rocks and steer us past them. But the wheels began to slip some more no matter where I turned, and there was a feeling in the front like the wheels were lifting slightly when I gunned the engine.

"Hey," Reid said, popping open the door in the back. "I'm getting out of this thing."

So now I was alone in the Humvee. This was unbelievable. The guys in my team out there walking up the mountain. Me in the Humvee feeling pretty confident the truck was about to flip over.

"You guys are fucking pussies!" I yelled.

No one contradicted me. No one volunteered to get back in the Humvee, either.

Whatever happened to moral support?

My legs started to tremble, and I clutched the steering wheel. Sweaty palms made a firm grip theoretical. Quinn was in front of the truck, waving right, waving left, doing something *useful*. I couldn't see Reid. Maybe when the truck flipped, it would flip right onto his lousy ass. Now, that would be poetic.

Things kept on in this vein for longer than I care to imagine—or remember. Up and up the damned mountain, my two team members safely out of harm's way. I'd downshifted into lowlock, and we made it up eventually. Quinn yanked big rocks from in front of the wheels sometimes. I swear the front tires lost touch with the ground once or twice when I pressed hard on the pedal.

Honestly, I thought this was the end of me.

Finally, though, when we arrived at the site, the FISTers were grinning. Said they'd been watching us through binos the whole way up. Said they were betting *for sure* we'd flip it. Surprised to find a girl behind the wheel.

"You going to help set up?" Sergeant Quinn asked.

"Are you fucking kidding?" I said. I was shaking so bad I could barely stand.

The other team cracked up laughing—but I could tell right away that they were laughing with me, not at me. I had won their respect by driving while the guys walked.

"Can I have a cigarette?" I asked them. I had been trying to quit smoking for a few weeks, but this drive tore my resolve.

"Boobs," a FISTer said, like it was some genuine insight. "Look, this one's got *boobs*."

The locals came to visit us on the mountain almost every day. Their visits livened things up. Only the men and boys; we never saw a single woman or girl. Full of curiosity about our stuff, they wandered onto our site while herding sheep and goats. Some stuck around for hours, asking if they could have a look through our binos at their houses in the valley far below. They made plain their gratitude for our presence. How delighted they were that

Americans had liberated Iraq! How grateful they were that Saddam Hussein had been pushed from power! Everyone had a story about how Saddam made their lives worse. How hopeful they were that our presence in their mountains meant there would soon be schools for their children, schools for kids who had never gone to school. So basically, they wanted us to stay— forever, if we liked.

These locals were Yezidis. They observed a religion that was not Islam. So far as I could gather, it was a nature-based religion that may predate not only Christianity but Judaism as well, and it also seemed to involve angels. They expressed an affinity with Israel I found surprising. They were not Kurdish, they told us, although Kurdish was their language.

We communicated with signs and gestures, but a few also spoke a little Arabic. So we communicated a little in broken Arabic as well. They visited so often that we soon counted on their visits and prepared presents for them in exchange for the presents they brought us.

They were an amazingly generous people despite their brutal poverty. They brought us tea, flat bread, and goat yogurt. When I asked for vegetables, they brought garlic, onions, tomatoes, cucumbers. They also brought butter and eggs—and once turkey eggs, which were amazing. The Yezidis fed me far better than my own unit did. For this I was immensely thankful. (Around this time I found a scale and discovered how dramatic my weight loss had been.) So the Yezidis brought me food, and we gave them old magazines, fruit, water, some MREs. For their wives and daughters I sometimes gave them a toothbrush and toothpaste— or hand lotion, shampoo, conditioner, deodorant, and dental floss. The concept behind some of these last items proved tough

At my graduation from Basic Combat Training at Fort Jackson, South Carolina, September 2000.

Studying Arabic at DLI, 2001.

Outside of the barracks at DLI.

Above: Heavy sandstorms during the GAC (Ground Assault Convoy) and at FARP Shell made the visibility difficult.

Left: Getting to know some locals in Dohuk.

Relaxing in the hammock in the back of our ISG's Humvee, spring 2003.

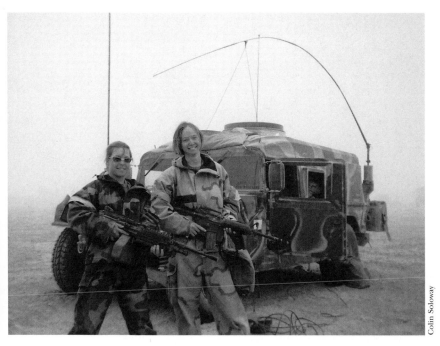

During a break on the GAC.

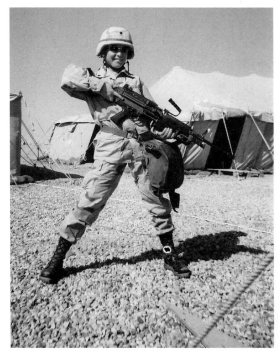

Our smallest team member carrying our team's biggest weapon.

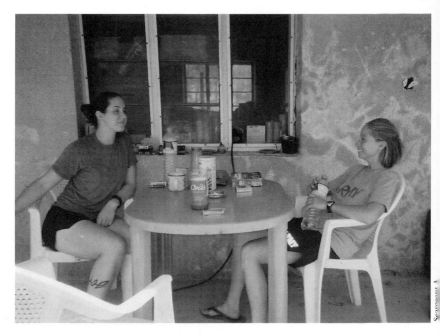

Relaxing during a brief visit to a friend's site.

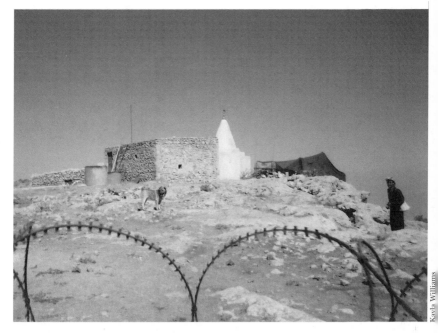

The Shrine at the second mountain site. A local and his dog, as seen from behind our C-Wire (Concertina wire), summer 2003.

Kayla Williams

Above: Guys on the COLT team reverify their zeros (check the accuracy of their weapon sights).

Right: Winds at the shrine atop Mt. Sinjar got strong enough to knock our antenna down—and make my hair crazy!

Justin Edgecombe

WILLIAMS U.S.ARMY

Justin Edgecombe

Rock climbing on Mt. Sinjar, summer 2003.

Above: One of the locals who brought me food looks at *Hustler.*

Left: Feeding Rak Hammer, the dog we doted on for months, during summer 2003.

Kayla Williams

I played with a puppy on the floor of our building at Range 54, the first time I lived indoors since leaving Kuwait, fall 2003.

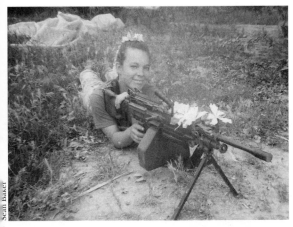

Down time in
Baghdad, 2003.

I get pinned—my Sergeant
rank is pinned on when I get
promoted— December 2003.

Christmas in Tal Afar—our company poses with "Santa."

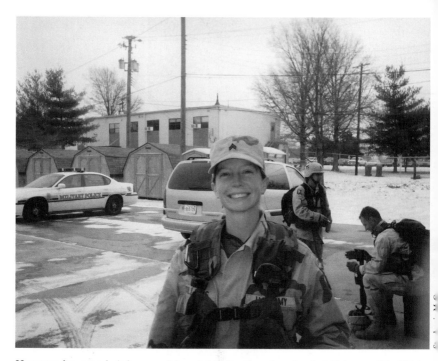

Happy to have made it home safely—right after the plane landed, February 8th, 2004.

Brian McGough

Dressed up for a big night out back in Tennessee.

to explain in Arabic. One day, for instance, I watched this Yezidi guy apply deodorant directly to his shirt.

Jasu, a man about my age, came more frequently than the rest. He liked to ask me about the United States, a place he hoped to move to someday. America held endless fascination for him. Especially, I soon realized, the very different ways that men and women behave in the West.

Leafing through an old *Newsweek* one day, Jasu pointed to a cigarette advertisement. It was a photograph of a girl and a guy in swimsuits strolling on a beach holding hands.

"In America you see this?" he asked.

By this point I knew he didn't mean the *beach*. He meant the bikini the girl wore.

"Sure you see it. In the summer, when it's hot. Like now. You see it all the time."

Jasu reflected.

"And holding hands. You can do this?"

"Yes. You can hold hands."

Then he branched out.

"And women—they go to the cinema in America? Even when they are married?"

"Yes. Married women go to the movies."

"I want to go to America," Jasu announced. "Find another wife. A better wife."

A FISTer wandered over and dropped another magazine into Jasu's lap.

"Maybe she's in here, Jasu. Your better wife."

Jasu was so delighted he dropped *Newsweek* in the dirt. Who needed girls in swimsuits? He happily let me photograph him with this new discovery: a back issue of *Hustler* magazine.

Welcome to America.

Some other day, he and I talked about life in the mountains.

I rambled: "It's so beautiful here. So peaceful. So far from the world. You live in a special and amazing place. Your life is so simple. You're so lucky. You don't have to worry about so many things."

I went on like this.

Jasu looked at me. Softly: "We have no electricity."

He was way too polite. What he meant to say was: "Don't go and romanticize my poverty, my isolation, my 'exotic' existence. What I want is what you Americans already have: opportunities, a car, a television, an education for my little brother. Money."

A week after we colocate at the mountain site with the FISTers, Geoff pulls rank on me.

"Don't take this the wrong way," SGT Quinn begins, but it's no great way to start. "I've been reviewing your logs. Doing some counts. Checking to see who's doing what. And it's clear . . . um . . . that you're not . . . *productive* enough."

Not take this the wrong way? What way am I *supposed* to take this?

"What are you talking about, Sergeant?"

He's nervous, but he doesn't back down.

"The tally. Your shifts don't tally. You're not making the count. Not making the cut. I don't want you to take this the wrong way—"

"Sergeant," I start to say, astonished.

"I'm going to sit sidesaddle your next shift."

"Wha—"

"Today. Fourteen hundred."

This is so bullshit and so unexpected I'm blinking back tears, and I turn away. I am not going to let this bastard see me like this. Not now. Not ever.

Quinn's got me, and he knows it. And he's not done. He turns back.

"And Williams," he says. "One more thing. This—*fraternizing*. With the other team. Those guys over there." He juts his chin in the general direction of the FISTers. "I think . . . well . . . it's my opinion that it's not so great for our team's integrity."

So that's it. I get it now, suddenly. Quinn is *jealous*.

Tears switch clear to anger.

"Listen, Sergeant," I say, as calmly as I can manage. "You do your job, I'll do my job. We're all stuck out here together, right? Let's make it work, okay? I've got no problem with how you're doing things. Let me do things my own way." I let him take this in. "And—what I do and who I do it with when I'm off shift is my own fucking business, okay?"

"Grow up," is what I want to say. But I leave it.

"Fine," he responds after a moment. "I'm still going to be there on your next shift."

"Whatever," I say, but I'm definitely unnerved at how deeply his petty disrespect of my professionalism ticks me off.

I'm feeling shaken and ill. Why? Why is it I can watch a man die and not freak out? Then I have a powerful physical reaction to a small—and *completely* unjustified—hassle from a superior? I go to see Staff Sergeant Gardner, and he responds blandly that he'll take care of Quinn. Which, of course, he does not do beforehand. Which leaves me to deal with Quinn there on shift to determine why my numbers are allegedly low. Which they are not. I go through the logs and prove that I'm right. Halfway through, Staff Sergeant Gardner pulls Sergeant Quinn aside, and nothing like this happens again. But I still fume from the insult.

It all totally sucks.

Why do I feel so damned helpless and *vulnerable* at moments like this?

If I were a FISTer, I think I'd punch Quinn in the face.

Which is weird because Quinn and I had been getting along pretty well before this happened. We'd gone hiking together a couple of times in the mountains at this site. We'd been talking more, too. Talking about music. Talking about relationships. But after this incident about my "productivity," I am not in the mood to hang with Geoff much anymore. I start hiking with the COLT guys and spend a lot more time with them.

A few days later at the OP, there's a little FIST party in progress. One more Saturday night. The sun is going down, and in the distance you can see the sparkling lights of both Syria and Turkey. A fine backdrop for the festivities. Quinn, SSG Gardner, Reid— they don't hang out with us much. Which makes the gathering even better.

A bonfire crackles. There's chicken (purchased from a Yezidi eager for U.S. currency) cooking in goat butter and Mrs. Dash. I don't eat meat, but it's smelling really good. Also: I shouldn't say it, but someone's got vodka in cans from the locals. I'm offered a swig or three.

Why not? It stings going down and has an odor like turpentine. Probably tastes like turpentine, though I can't say, never having tried turpentine. Mixed with Gatorade the vodka's okay, though it's got one hell of a kick. Certainly beats teetotaling after so many months.

"Hey, Boobs," Hodgson says. He never quits calling me this after that first day. "My wife tells me she's taking my paycheck and buying herself fake boobs for when I get home. What do you think of that?"

All the FISTers tell me Hodgson is one scary redneck none of them would ever want to fight. They tell me Hodgson, the youngest of four brothers, had to learn early how to hold his own. They tell me about the time Hodgson beat the shit out of Travis. Knocked Travis's head into a big van door that almost cut his ear off. No one exactly sure what Travis said to Hodgson to deserve this.

"Your wife *needs* boobs, man," someone says. "I've seen your wife."

"Says who?" Hodgson's had a head start on the canned vodka. Unclear how long he's been downing shots. "What's wrong with my wife's boobs? Anyway, I was planning on a new gun with the extra money I'm getting here. Fuck if she thinks she can get cosmetic surgery with it. I like her the way she is. I like her small boobs."

"Hey. Look at me." It's Matt Crowther, another FISTer, rotating his groin obscenely against a Humvee. "I'm fucking a tire just thinking about Hodgson's wife's new boobs."

"Better than humping that sheep," Travis says. "What were you thinking about then? That was too much."

"Hey, that sheep was hot." Matt looks my way, right hand on his crotch.

"Hey. Keep passing that can around!"

"What gets you hot?" It's Matt to me.

"Small dicks. Unmanly men." I look around. "You guys."

"Screw you, hatchet wound."

This talk gives me a nasty shiver.

"Fuck off, peanut prick."

That gets a small guffaw from Hodgson.

"At least with blue medicated foot powder on my nuts," Matt opines, "it's real cool down there when the breeze blows through."

None of them wears underwear, and their pants are ripped in the groin from never changing clothes for weeks on end. None of them knows how to sew.

"Listen now," Travis says. "What's the difference between a hooker and an onion?"

"Ah, that's my joke," I complain, passing the can to him. "No one ever cried when they cut a hooker. Hey. What's the first thing a woman does when she gets back from a battered women's shelter?"

None of them know.

"The dishes, if she's smart."

The alcohol makes the night hazy.

It's easy to judge our adolescent behavior, harder to realize how hard it is to pass the time. Understand: There is *nothing* for us to do.

This is a listening post/operations post (LP/OP). Our Prophet team is the LP; we run twenty-four-hour operations with a four-person team. That means each of us works six hours a day. This gets broken down into two three-hour shifts. We are doing our mission, which is intercept and direction-find on enemy communications. The rest of the time we just sit there. Meanwhile the FISTers watch the border. What I see them do is take notes on the number of vehicles that drive down the road across from Syria. From what I can gather, their main concern is watching for smugglers.

Basically, though, there is nothing to do. We are so desperate to find things to fill the time, we make up games kids in grade school would consider beneath them. Case in point: The FISTers throw rocks at one another and at me. For fun. They aim at my breasts. It's a game. They chuck stones at one another's groins. That's a big game. A major activity. The objective? Get a stone into those small aforementioned rips in a guy's pair of pants. Believe me, it is not easy. With practice, however, it *can* be done.

One day, not the night of the party, someone finds a beetle and decides to chuck it at Matt. The beetle actually gets into the hole in his pants. And clamps down on his penis. Matt panics, screeching like a little girl.

Our life on the mountain.

Other days we take hikes. The mountains are stunning, and hiking does qualify as exercise.

Out hiking, the guys develop more time-wasting activities. More stupid soldier tricks.

"You would *never* jump off that ledge."

"Say I won't?"

"You won't."

"Say I won't?"

"You won't."

Then you have to do it.

"You wouldn't throw a rock at Kayla's boobs now, would you?"

"Say I won't?"

"You won't."

"Say I won't?"

And they keep this up until someone does.

This foolishness eases its way into common parlance until it also works the other way around: You set up what you're going to do by introducing it yourself.

"Say I won't pop off a few rounds at that rock over there?"

"You won't."

"Say I won't?"

"You won't."

And then you do. In other words it isn't a dare so much as an idea you have, and then you provoke someone else to provoke you into doing it.

Juvenile? You bet it is. We're writing the book on juvenile.

One time Hodgson pops off a few rounds, then laughs.

"Say I won't set the mountain on fire with a tracer round?"

Too late. Hodgson does fire a tracer round that does hit a patch of dry grass that obligingly springs into flames. It's such a happy coincidence, Matt grabs his camera to photograph the mountain burning down.

"Holy shit!" It's Hodgson, incredulous at his dumb luck. "I set the side of the mountain on fire!"

Matt's taking pictures while the rest of us, gear bouncing on our backs, run down to snuff out the flames. Seems like I spend too much time in Iraq putting out friendly fires.

Speaking of which.

There's the time the FISTers' platoon sergeant—whom they *like,* by the way—visits the mountain site. Their leadership makes these periodic visits, checking in to see what's up and to resupply food and water. Sometimes he's there overnight; sometimes he stays for a few days. Anyway, this one time their platoon sergeant is making the final ascent to the site. Maybe he's still a hundred meters off when someone suggests: "Say I won't fire a round down there just to get Kelly's attention?"

This is *beyond* wrong, even though the round is not close to him. Nothing personal, of course. Just another "Say I won't?"

Kelly could often be an asshole. A real cocksucker. He really got into the canned vodka and Gatorade. He'd been deployed to Bosnia, Kosovo, Afghanistan, and now Iraq. Like Lieutenant Samuels, Kelly had been part of Operation Anaconda in the mountains of Afghanistan, and even when I got to know him better, he never really wanted to talk about it. It was like a scale with soldiers. Those of us who'd been to Iraq had difficulty dealing with civilians when we got home; we tended to feel more comfortable with other soldiers who'd been deployed. Same thing with Anaconda: Many of them had little to say to those of us who'd only known deployment in Iraq. It just didn't count in the same way. The only difference with Kelly is that he acted out more than most. He got pretty angry, I think. And pretty drunk a lot of the time.

On the other hand he and I shared a lot of musical tastes. So that was a bond of sorts. So we'd talk about music, ideas, politics, books—things like that. We would have interesting conversations even though at the same time Kelly could be a real jackass. Literally, he'd say to me: "Fix me some eggs, bitch." And I'd fix him eggs. Because I'm retarded. Or nice. Or whatever.

Meeting Shane Kelly I was reminded how much women like assholes. How much I tended to like assholes over the years. How much a lot of women like men like Kelly—possibly because they believe that they deserve being treated badly.

The pop psychology theory goes: Women are drawn to men who are like their fathers. So if your father is moody, cold, and emotionally distant, women may tend to be drawn to men who are like that. Again with the pop psychology, you think that if you can win the love of a man like that, you are symbolically winning the love of the father that you never felt you really got. After I meet Shane Kelly, I begin sometimes to analyze myself in this way. But it also has very little to do with him; historically I've dated a lot of guys who treated me like shit.

At some point I think I really figure Kelly out. He will treat you like shit until you've proved that you can be trusted. He has walls just as I do, except that his are pretty thick, probably thicker than mine. So I see rather quickly that a lot of his talk has been just talk. And that he is not in fact a real asshole. That his asshole behavior toward me was a defense mechanism to protect himself from the possibility of pain.

It takes awhile, and it really doesn't happen until much later, but I begin to feel that I understand Shane. I learn a little about his fucked-up childhood; no dad, Mom raises the family by herself and has a predictably hard time. (At least until she remarries; Shane's stepdad is a wonderful man.) To this day Shane has had almost no contact at all with his father. Even later, when the shit really goes down, his father does nothing. Makes no effort to be in touch. And I know that this affects him. To be in a combat zone and your father does not send you even a damned postcard saying: "Hope you live." That has to have an emotional effect on him.

From what I understand, Shane has had a difficult military career. He's gotten in trouble a lot.

Not all his friends see Shane the way I do. Some of his friends tell me: "He doesn't treat you well enough. You can do better than that. You deserve better than that." Because Shane likes to talk like he's bad. He likes to mouth off. He likes to get drunk in bars and stir things up. Feel sorry for himself. So he ends up yelling at Army wives, calling them fat fucks or whatever. Blacks out and forgets how he got himself home.

Yeah, so his friends sometimes tell me I deserve better.

Things do get out of hand. Like one of the nights we drink canned vodka. A night Kelly happens not to be around.

"I gotta piss." It's Hodgson, but when he tries to stand up, he stumbles down again.

"Let me help you," says Matt, watching Hodgson sway. Hodgson doesn't object.

Well, sir, we were completely drunk on vodka purchased from the locals, and then . . . um . . . Hodgson slipped and fell off the mountain—

A difficult thing to explain to the wife. Or to the higher-ups.

So Matt braces Hodgson around the shoulders, and both of them move behind the truck. Shortly we hear them stumbling back.

"Just push me into her, man," Hodgson is whispering loud to Matt. "Push me into her."

"No way." Matt: Always sober. He never drinks at the mountain site, saying later that it was just too spooky. "Not happening. You do not want to do that."

"Just push me, man. Just push me into her."

"Push yourself, man. I'll have nothing to do with this."

They come back together, and Matt sits. Hodgson pretend-stumbles toward me. Before I can react, his hands are up, cupping my tits and squeezing. Hard.

"Mmm." His eyes are closed as he absorbs the sensation, while I shove him away.

"Whatever, dude," I say, slapping his hands. "Stupid redneck."

He's smiling.

"Thank you, Boobs," he mumbles.

"You're one sorry drunk bastard."

"Mmm." Now he's lost and stumbling again, his final ounce of strength consumed by the grope. Done for the night.

"Assholes." I generalize it. "All you guys."

"Ah, come on now. Don't get mad. We're like kittens. Stroke us. Make us purr."

"Let's play a game," Travis says. "Truth or dare."

"Not tonight."

"Some other night?"

"Whatever. I'm going to bed."

"Can we come with?"

"Why don't you jerk each other off? Isn't that what you usually do?"

Matt turns to Travis. "Wanna try?"

I'm gone before I hear an answer.

Sergeant Quinn gets set to go. His time is done. He's been accepted into the Army's Green-to-Gold program. They plan to pay for him to attend college; he'll owe them several more years of his life—but as an officer. The bottom line is: He's heading home.

We'd been strained since Quinn got in my face about my "productivity." I wouldn't go out of my way to spend time with him, but it wasn't a really big deal. When we interacted in the vehicle, I still talked to him. Even after the incident when he criticized my work, Quinn continued to sit and talk with me when I was on shift. He kept me company. So we'd talk about all sorts of things during the three hours of my daytime shift. (I wonder if it offended him that I never stayed with him when *he* was on shift.)

"Listen," he says. "When I spoke to Sergeant Gardner about—"

"Forget it."

"No, I wanted to—"

"*Forget it.*" I pause for a moment. "But there's one thing I want to ask you."

"Yes?"

I confront Quinn right before he leaves.

"Why the hell won't the guys in our platoon ever talk to me anymore?" I ask. "Down at the airfield. What the fuck's going on? Why do they act like they all hate me?"

And Quinn tells me because he knows he won't have to deal with the consequences.

"They think you're a big whore," Quinn says, looking away. "They think you're a slut. And they don't want to have anything to do with you. Because they think you're a slut."

"I don't get it."

"Listen," Quinn says. "I think I know what this is all about. Remember? Right before we deployed? You were having sex with Connelly, right? The guys think that makes you a big slut."

This makes zero sense to me. And I am getting very angry about it.

"Connelly was the only guy I ever fucked at Fort Campbell before we deployed," I say to Quinn. "From when I got there in July until we left, he was the only one. So what the hell . . ."

Then I put it together. The only thing I can think is that I tried briefly dating this guy while I had been at Campbell. But it hadn't worked out. I'd told the guy I was messed up in the head because I'd just gotten divorced.

"I'm not in a place where I can give you an emotional connection," I told this guy. "At all."

And the guy said: "That's fine."

So we were just dating. We never even had sex.

Then at a party at Sergeant Biddle's house, I got really drunk and fucked Connelly.

So this other guy I'm dating, his feelings got hurt, and he got upset about it. For three days. And then he got over it. And we remained friends. We are still friends today.

But the guys in my platoon acted all pissed off. They decided I was a slut or a whore, that I cheated on the guy I was dating. They probably did not even know I never slept with this other guy. They just assumed that if a man and a woman are together, they must be having sex.

So they decided to make this big bullshit judgment on me. And it was really painful. Because I had gone through a situation in high school when I definitely fucked too many guys. I admit that. I'm not proud of it. I got treated horribly. People said vicious things about me when I was in high school. People called me a slut all the time. People were very cruel, and it was tough. I'd been sexually assaulted when I was thirteen—that definitely messed with my sense of control over my own body and my ability to make choices about my own sexuality. But that's over half my lifetime ago by now. And I spent a lot of those years trying to get over feeling crappy for things I'd done when I was a kid.

Now here I am in Iraq being made to feel crappy all over again for things I did *not* do at Fort Campbell. Because at Fort Campbell I was basically responsible. I was basically good. And here these guys are treating me like I'm some dirty slut. It is very upsetting. It brings back a lot of unpleasant memories.

"Yeah," Quinn says, taking it all in.

"And Connelly? He was fucking some sixteen-year-old girl while he was seeing me. But *I'm* the big whore?"

"I know," Quinn says.

"So there's nothing wrong with him, right? He can fuck this sixteen-year-old and fuck me or fuck any other girl he wants at the same time—and there's nothing wrong with him, right?"

"Yeah," Quinn says.

"But if I even *talk* to one guy while I'm fucking another guy, I'm this fucking dirty whore?"

"Yeah," Quinn says.

"Damn them," I say. "They're just jealous because they never got any fucking ass. I think they're just afraid of women. They never get any action, so I'm the slut? Assholes!"

"Time for me to go," Quinn says. "I just thought you should know."

"Yeah," I say.

We hug. It's the one time we ever have any physical contact in all the time I've known him.

I should be glad Quinn's leaving, but I'm not. I feel disappointed. As much of a snot as Quinn sometimes was, I still know I'll miss him.

We went through combat together. Quinn brought me Gatorade when he found out I'd watched a guy die. It was a minor thing, but it meant something to me.

And I'd been able to admit my self-doubts to Quinn. That's not easy for me. I'd opened up to Quinn, and he'd been okay with it. He'd been okay with me. He told me I was a good person, which sounds cheesy but meant a lot to me at the time.

With Lauren gone, Quinn was the only member of my team

with whom I could actually be vulnerable. The only remaining member of my team with whom I had any sort of emotional bond or relationship at all. And now he was going.

The FISTers tried to make up for Hodgson groping me by procuring more food than I could possibly imagine. The halal meals my unit *claimed* it could not find in-country, the FISTers began to get me by the case.

But that was not all. Somehow they procured lots of everything: cases of shelf-stable milk, boxes of cereal, cases of fruit, boxes of banana chips, reams of Nutri-Grain bars, packages of chocolate milk, boxes of condiments, packets of peanut butter and jelly, shelf-stable bread. We're talking *tons* of food. I was not stuck sucking on MREs any longer, watching my entire body fat evaporate. Add all this to the wonderful stuff I got every day from the Yezidis, and I was over my involuntary weight-loss program.

Every morning we called in a report of our supplies. Fuel, ammo, everything we had. And this one morning I got to the report on our food supply.

I said: "We've got a whole shitload of food and water."

"What? Sorry. That won't do."

"Look," I said into the radio. "It's a whole shitload."

"I say again: We need a *count*."

"Okay. Wait one."

So I went and counted. And counted. And counted. And came back to the radio.

"We're got ten cases of . . ." And I ran it down. Every last bit of it.

"Yeah," the guy said when I was finally done. "Roger that. You called it. That is a whole *shitload* of food and water."

I came to adore the mountain site. Up there for six weeks. The best six weeks of the war for me. I told myself someday I'd find my way back, if possible.

Late in June we got pulled from our Shangri-la back to 3rd Brigade for inventories.

Jasu came for a last visit, looking severely bummed.

"I'll miss you," he said.

"Yeah," I said. "Me too. I'll miss you, too."

"One favor?"

"What?"

He pointed to a stack of empty cardboard boxes.

"Cardboard?" I asked. "What about it?"

"For my house," he said, sounding hopeful.

The last time we saw them, Jasu and his donkey were hauling away as many cardboard boxes as possible.

For a floor. For his house.

FREE MARKET

We moved to a second site on the other side of the same mountain. I was now the only person left on the team that had been there from the beginning. It felt awkward, the constantly shifting personnel.

The only thing that kept me going was the COLT team that relocated with us to this new site. This time, however, we were colocated with others, and the absence of relative privacy sucked. There was a far more crowded scene up there, with probably twenty soldiers around all the time. There was a ground surveillance radar team. There were four retransmission teams spread out about a hundred meters away across the road from us, and they were okay. But there was not a whole lot for them to do, either. Their equipment picked up a signal and retransmitted it so the signal could go farther; once they had it in place they didn't actually have to do anything for the equipment to work. Unless it stopped working. All that was left for the team to do was sit back and let the radios do their thing. They were not pushing buttons for it to operate; it happened automatically.

Efforts were made to make friends. Do the sociable thing. But I didn't really feel into it. I got invitations to cross the road to play cards or watch a VCD, but more often than not I declined. I don't know why. At the first mountain site I guess I got used to being more alone—or alone with the FISTers, and I was not as eager now to reach out.

Let me explain something about the FISTers.

Maybe it sounds like they were jerks who hated girls and liked to talk us down. And I would say to that: They were, but they weren't.

In the real world, guys bond through competition. They play football games. They play video games. They verbally spar. They throw rocks at one another. Guys like to try and establish a hierarchy. They jockey for who's on top.

Now, I can play that game. I tried to play it with Staff Sergeant Gardner, and he was probably better at it than I am. I can play it with guys who value intelligence. But I can only sort of play it with guys like the FISTers. It's not the same with them.

The FISTers would talk trash with me to bond with me.

They wouldn't talk trash with me if they didn't like me. If we weren't friends. Put it this way: They would never have insulted me all the time if I had been only a stranger to them.

Matt and I wrestled. This was definitely a guy thing to do. But we tussled on the mountain.

And the FISTers would yell out: "Hey Matt, you got beat up by a girl!"

Matt would yell back: "No, I didn't! I won!"

The FISTers also always gave me credit when I deserved credit. They would always tell me: "You're really smart. You're smarter than we are."

And I'd give them credit, too. I would tell them: "Sure, I've read more books than you guys. I can speak Arabic. But I couldn't fix my truck if my life depended on it. I know nothing about engines. I would never be able to understand your equipment. You are all smarter than I am about how to make things work."

Being around these guys and military personnel in general had given me a whole new appreciation for nonintellectual skills. These were people with manual skills. They knew how to use their hands. They were not afraid to get sweaty or dirty. And I respected them for it.

Tensions at this site only arose when one of the retrans teams informed our squad leader that we'd have to pull guard shift with them and watch the road. The retrans guys periodically started up the truck so the battery didn't die. But that was really it. Plus pull guard.

We, on the other hand, had to *work* on our shifts. And we were on shift twenty-four hours a day. For us pulling guard meant ninety minutes more shift time a day, on top of our regular shifts. It was a minor gripe, but under the circumstances it took on much bigger importance. Our team had been in-country now for nearly six months working seven days a week running ops twenty-four hours a day. No break. No vacation. No time away from the people, the mission, anything. No such thing as a *weekend*. And so it was the small shit that began to drive us crazy. And this request to pull guard meant even less sleep than we were already getting.

At this point we'd lost Sergeant Quinn, so the three of us each worked two four-hour shifts a day. My shifts for a long time were 10:00 A.M. to 2:00 P.M. and 10:00 P.M. to 2:00 A.M. So I might sleep from 2:30 in the morning (since it always took a while to wind down after a shift) until the sun would hit me and wake me up around 8:00 A.M. That meant between five and six hours of sleep a day, which never felt like enough.

I coped with existence mainly by getting away on hikes. Rock climbing with my M-4 was not easy— it totally threw off my balance. But I did it, and it was great to get away with one or more of the FISTers for a few hours. I tended to go hiking with Matt. But I also hiked occasionally with Travis. I went hiking with Rivers once, and also Bill, our civilian linguist. Technically, at least according to those at higher levels, this walking away from base was probably not permitted, but on-site no one challenged us. So we'd go, wandering wherever. We carried handheld radios, and we were always in range of communication. It felt like a good thing to become more familiar with the area.

Mainly if we came across locals, the locals were Yezidis. I continued to be overwhelmed by their amazing generosity.

Their Arabic was not great, and whatever Kurdish we spoke was limited to a few basic phrases, so conversations tended toward the most common of denominators. And after a time there was a remarkable degree of repetition in these little talks with the Yezidis we met.

On one hike we came to a small Yezidi dwelling in the mountains, and the men practically pulled us over to sit down with them.

Matt and Bill and I sat awkwardly around on the ground while the men watched us, and one prepared tea. These were very poor farming people. They grew pomegranates and grapes and some vegetables. The men told us that they stayed there in the summer months; in the winter they lived in the village below with their families.

Then this one local with a handlebar mustache placed three glasses before us, and there weren't enough glasses to go around. So we drank tea while they sat there. They offered us grapes. And then he got out a raw onion that he chopped into quarters, and laid the pieces out for us. He then sprinkled some coarsely ground salt on a plate, and also set down a large piece of flat bread.

We looked at one another, and then down at the raw onion slices. And then again at one another.

"Eat," the man said in Arabic.

I said, "It's a raw onion."

"Eat. Eat." The man was not understanding our hesitation.

"It's a raw onion," I repeated.

"Yes. You dip it in the salt and eat it with bread."

The guys were really not sure about this.

"You're kidding me?" one of them said.

"No. Eat it."

So we ate it to be polite. And it wasn't that bad, though it was nothing I would serve as an appetizer back home.

Then, as always, I had the obligatory conversation I had with all the Yezidis. No matter what, no matter when, it was always the same conversation, and it went something like this:

"We are Yezidis," the Yezidi man began.

"Yes." I had heard this before, and knew precisely where it was heading. "Yes. I know. You are Yezidis."

"Do you know of the Yezidis in America?"

"No," I would be feeling weary already. "No. Nobody in America has heard of the Yezidis."

"Will you tell the Americans about us?"

"Yes. I will do my best."

"We are *not* Muslims."

"I know. I got it. You're *not* Muslims. You're Yezidis."

"We are like Jews. And we are like Christians. But we are *not* like Muslims."

"Yes. I know." Yes, everyone here told me the same thing. "Yes, I've got it."

"We love Americans because you hate Muslims. And we hate Muslims, too. So that's why we love Americans. And we want America to stay here forever. You—or Israel. To protect us from the Muslims. Because they cut down our fig trees and stole our women."

"Okay." I did not want to start a debate here or an argument, but I wanted to be clear. "We don't hate Muslims," I began. "That's really . . . um . . . not the point. We don't hate any religion. And we're here so that you can have a democracy. And so you can have freedom. And in a democracy everybody gets to help decide how to run the government and how to run the country. And even the Yezidis can help. You can participate in the new government under a democracy. Because you're going to have freedom. That's why we're here, to help establish freedom and democracy. And then we're going to *leave*."

"No, no." He waved away this speech, as if it was foolish or irrelevant. And he spoke now as if to someone who was a trifle dense. "No. It will never work. This would never happen. Americans have to stay here *forever*." He paused. "Or Israel."

"Israel is never going to come." Now it was my turn to make a point that seemed too obvious to mention. "Let me tell you. Israel will never be here. They will never be in Iraq. They will never establish anything here. I promise you. They are not coming."

Somehow these conversations were on a tape loop, and it began again at the beginning.

"We are like Christians. We are like Jews. We hate the Muslims. *Like you*."

"No. We *don't* hate the Muslims—"

"Will you please tell Mr. Bush about the Yezidis?"

I guess the thinking here was that I was not getting it. So they might as well go right to the top. Get the president involved, since this soldier was not grasping the issues.

"I don't know him." I said this as politely as I could.

"Will you write him a letter? Will you call him? Will you tell Mr. Bush? Does Mr. Bush know about the Yezidis?"

"I do not know what Mr. Bush knows about the Yezidis."

"Tell Mr. Bush. Tell Mr. Bush about the Yezidi people. Because we are good people."

"Yes, you are. You are good people. You're generous and kind and friendly people. You give me food all the time. You're very nice. You're very kind. I love the Yezidis."

"Tell Mr. Bush."

"Yeah. All right. Yes. I am going to write Mr. Bush a letter and tell him how great you are."

"Thank you. Thank you."

After our little picnic, we took pictures of the men and their donkey. Then this guy with the handlebar mustache—he was about fifty years old—led us back up the mountain. And he scampered up the mountain in plastic sandals like a goddamn gazelle. Here we were, thinking we're bad-ass Army soldiers, but we couldn't keep up.

And the very next time I met a Yezidi, I had almost the identical conversation all over again. Word for word.

One day these random young people just showed up at our site.

"Hey," they called out to us.

"Hey." What the fuck was going on?

One kid was from Chicago, and started talking to Matt about

growing up in Illinois. He was thinking about possibly attending college in Matt's hometown. But Matt was trying to dissuade him.

"Nah," Matt told this one American teenager. "I wouldn't go there. You can't watch your cornhole that much."

Turned out these kids were volunteers from some Christian group, and they'd all come there to assist the Iraqis.

So we pulled out a bunch of MREs and served lunch for these American kids. But they were having trouble eating out of the pouches like we did. Luckily we happened to have some paper plates; that worked. And the soldiers began to explain how to make the MREs.

We were stoked. We hadn't seen real people in forever.

Matt got all cute.

"Oh, let me help you with that. Let me get that for you."

The kids had come up our way to see the Yezidi shrine. Check out all the great sites of Iraq.

Here's a trash pile! Here's a destroyed tank! There's another rabid dog!

We had the only healthy grown dog in Iraq. The FISTers named her Rak Hammer. She'd been beaten a lot and hated Iraqis. She'd been adopted and then left at the site by the Pathfinders, and when they rolled out, she stayed with the fire support team.

It was a violation of General Order No. 1 to keep pets or mascots. Pets were specifically outlawed—like porn and liquor. But almost everyone we knew in Iraq had a pet of some kind. I knew people who had a cat, a hedgehog, a falcon, and lots of people who had dogs.

Packs of wild dogs roam Iraq, and some are rabid. In Mosul

soldiers would even go on dog-eradication projects and shoot dogs. This was hard for a lot of soldiers to do.

Dogs in Iraq that soldiers adopted often hated the locals with a deep and abiding passion. The locals tended to throw rocks at dogs. And beat them. While we fed them and were friendly to them. So our dog made a big ruckus when locals approached. Which proved convenient. She also became very protective of her territory and kept all the other local dogs away from us. She became fiercely loyal because we treated her well.

We also had a little puppy. One day I was told an older dog killed the puppy—which was an unpleasant thing. (Though I learned more than a year later that it was Sergeant Kelly who accidentally killed the puppy. He'd thrown it up into the air, and it fell hard onto the rocks below. It was maimed, so he killed it.)

Our pets were extremely important for morale. Our dogs became a pretty big part of our lives. I took a lot of pictures of our damned dog.

The Army puts out an informal policy against physical contact. Even though the Army is one of the few environments in the States in which men can touch each other and it's okay. Guys pat each other on the ass all the time in the Army. It's called a "good game." Guys can also half hug each other; not front hug, but a little side shoulder hug. That's perfectly manly and acceptable. If two men in civilian clothes hugged like this it might be considered gay. But Army guys can do it whenever they want—because they're Army. Real tough guys.

But physical contact was more or less something I did not have during my deployment. Guys were extra careful not to touch me. As a female I was not really a part of the "good game."

So having pets around was important for this reason: Here was a creature I could touch and love.

The Yezidi shrine at this mountain site was a small rock building with objects dangling from the ceiling. There were little alcoves in the shrine where locals placed offerings and worshipped. People came and left money that anyone else could take, if someone else came who needed it more. Or people took the money to use toward the upkeep of the shrine itself. And inside the shrine there was another door to a smaller room that I never entered or saw. No one exactly explained the purpose of the shrine, but we sometimes heard accusations from local Muslims that the Yezidis were *devil worshippers*. The dangling objects appeared to have more to do with the rays of the sun, but nothing was made clear.

One day a father came to worship with his several children, and the oldest daughter in the family appeared mesmerized by me.

She was excited to see a female American because she could talk to me. It was not appropriate for her to speak to the men, but she was permitted to speak to me. And it was the first time I encountered a young local woman with whom I could spend some time talking.

She didn't know how old she was, since the locals didn't have a real way to record birthdays, but she estimated that she was about sixteen.

Our conversations were extremely stilted, given her near-absence of Arabic and my difficulty making myself understood as a result.

Her name was Leila, and we became friendly, if not friends.

She returned to the shrine with her family three or four more times while I was there, and we began to exchange gifts.

The mother never joined her family on this pilgrimage.

I noticed that all the girls in the family had tattoos on their faces, but none more than Leila. Small dots on her chin, her forehead, and the sides of her face.

I tried to ask what these dots on her face meant, but there was too much of a language barrier. The only thing I could ascertain was that the girls seemed to receive more of these tattoos as they grew up; Leila's youngest sister had no markings on her face, but her other sisters had one, two, and four as they got older. But whether the dots were religious or cultural, I never learned.

At another time in Iraq, when we were among the Bedouin people, I noticed from a distance that the women appeared to have tattooed writing on their feet. But again I never learned what it meant; I also never got close enough to the Bedouin women to read the tattoos. I was always very curious.

Besides my general interest in the locals, and my desire to get to know what the civilians were like, it was just great to see a girl. This was such a male environment otherwise. And even though our conversations were hobbled by our mutual inability to make ourselves easily understood, there was just a sense of *relief*. For me. And, I began to suspect, for Leila as well.

Jimmy the Ice Man has arrived. Are we glad to see him!

No one knows his real name, or how he first found out we are up here, but everyone calls him Jimmy the Ice Man. The "Ice Man" part is easy: Jimmy brings us slabs of ice he buys down in the village. Jimmy is probably Kurdish or maybe Yezidi; we don't know that, either. We also don't know where "Jimmy" came from; probably some smart-ass soldier's sense of humor that stuck. Anyway, Jimmy is an awesome guy who has quickly and efficiently mastered the skills of the marketplace. We respect this about him. We respect how quickly he has found a market, and how he knows immediately how to exploit it.

The arrangement goes something like this: First Jimmy hires a taxi for the whole day for five dollars. He then loads the taxi with consumer goods—anything and everything he thinks he can sell to a captive American military audience stuck out in the god-forsaken wilderness with little to do and absolutely nothing on which to spend its money. Jimmy starts with the essentials. There's the ice, of course. By this point in the summer we are talking temperatures of a hundred degrees most days, even in the mountains. The ice is very nice, especially when combined with the cases of soda Jimmy hauls to us in his rented taxi. It's a great combination. Buy the ice, and buy the soda to chill on the ice. Prices are reasonable, given that Jimmy is sole vendor for our AO (area of operations). We fully recognize that Jimmy is pulling in a huge profit margin, but we respect and admire his ingenuity. Big slabs of ice about two or three feet long and six inches across that he'd pick up for a quarter. And he'd charge us three dollars. An amazing mark-up on all the same stuff we could get way cheaper at base does not appear unreasonable to us under the circumstances.

"Hey, Jimmy! You got that shit we talked about last time!"

From this basic plan of action, Jimmy gets ambitious. Branches out. He begins to take orders. Anything he can get his hands on, he will happily serve as mule. He wants his customers happy, and he works the crowd to make sure folks are satisfied with the service.

This means lots of business. Soldiers wanting just about anything you can imagine. Cigarettes, gifts for girlfriends or wives, knives, lighters, soccer jerseys, propane tanks, prayer beads—you name it. (Personally, I buy a lot of scarves.) Most of it is junk, but we purchase it. Happy to keep Jimmy happy. Happy to have something, anything, to distract us from the routineness of our routine.

The local kids have been bringing us food almost every day since we got to this new site. All sorts of good stuff. Two kinds of eggplants (green and purple), green peppers, tomatoes, cucumbers, potatoes, onions, eggs—it's their offering to us. Their welcome to the American liberators. They have no sense of what their food should cost, so they start asking for small change. Maybe a dollar. No big deal. We meet their monetary demands with a chuckle.

As Jimmy continues his trips up the mountain with a taxiload of goodies, though, the children grow bolder. Wanting more money for their product. And then they begin to jack up the prices. Two dollars for a bag of vegetables. Then three dollars. Five dollars. And upward. Testing out what the market will bear.

Some of the guys get pissed. They start saying things you'd rather not hear them say. But it's not like we all don't have similar thoughts at one time or another. "Get these fucking locals away from me" or "I'm tired of them asking me for water" or "I'm tired of them asking me for money" or "I don't want to deal with these fucking people." And you understand this attitude after a while. After all these kids are *always* underfoot. Always wanting something. And am I really going to fork over five bucks for some damned eggplants the size of my fist?

Finally we refuse to deal with them, and the situation normalizes. Someone speaks to the kids. Settles them down. Still, you can't help but take note of how *fast* the free market has taken root out here in the Kurdish mountains.

Jimmy the Ice Man is a real character. I love this guy. And he provides some memorable moments.

Like the time he brings us Osama bin lighters. Picture this. A butane lighter with the image of Osama bin Laden and the Twin Towers in New York City. And there's a plane flying into the Twin Towers. And a little red light. When you press down, the light glows red. It's an instant classic. Every soldier wants one. It is gruesome and morbid, but it also reminds us of where we are— and why. (Or at least what our fearless leaders wanted us to think about why we are here; we all knew there was no connection between the war in Iraq and 9/11. We talked about it all the time.) Or how about the lighter shaped like a heart? And it has the faces of both George W. Bush and Saddam Hussein. And the top of the lighter is a fighter plane. Very strange. (Made in China. What's up with that?)

I loved this about Jimmy. That he does this. Capitalism in its purest form.

Sometimes, though, Jimmy's entrepreneurial spirit goes a little too far, and we have to set some boundaries. Or at least I do.

"No, Jimmy," I'm telling him for the umpteenth time. "I do not need *dresses*. I do not need *skirts*."

"Skirts for you," Jimmy says in surprisingly good English, pushing a stack of fabrics closer to make sure I am not misunderstanding that this is a special deal he wishes to make. "No one else. You."

"No, Jimmy," I say. "Thank you for . . . um . . . your interest. Thank you. But no."

"But who else?" He smiles. But he is also disappointed; I can tell. "Who else will wear such things here?" He gestures to all the guys at this site. I am the only woman.

"I don't know," I say. *But I haven't asked you to bring me clothes!*

"Look, Jimmy," I try to explain. "Thank you for your interest. And the effort. But I am not allowed to wear anything but my uniform." I point to my uniform. I try to make *this* the point, as if I too am disappointed that I am not going to be able to model these clothes which are, in fact, beyond hideous. Their bright array of mismatched colors defies easy characterization.

Jimmy is not easily dissuaded. He relents, but then next time he taxis up to us, he tries again. Same dresses. Same skirts.

On another occasion Jimmy wants to know how much we make as soldiers here in Iraq, working for the U.S. military. This is not a simple matter to explain to a man who must consider the fifty dollars he might make on a good day selling ice and soda to twenty Americans in the Sinjar Mountains a small fortune. So I try to make it make sense in a way I hope he can grasp.

"Two thousand dollars a month," I begin, and I see his eyes grow large with wonder. "But—but there are lots of costs involved."

"Costs?"

"Expenses. Back home. We have many things for which we must continue to pay. Even though we are living here. Like, for example, I own a house in America. And I have a mortgage. That's six hundred dollars a month right there. For the next thirty years. And I own a new car. That's three hundred dollars a month for the next five years."

Jimmy is quiet, calculating these expenses. And it's all true: I *am* underpaid. Soldiers of my rank and below with dependents qualify for food stamps. But I'm hardly done.

"And there are other things. Heat for the winter. And electricity. And home insurance and car insurance."

Jimmy is looking increasingly somber, studying me carefully as I itemize the costs of an ordinary American life.

"I just want you to understand—it's expensive." I'm on a roll. I'm almost convincing myself. "We make a lot of money—by the standards here. But—it's expensive. And there's more—"

"Food, telephone—" he interrupts.

"Yes, yes," I say. He gets it.

"Take it, please."

He is holding a can of soda out to me.

"For you. Please. *No cost.* Free soda. It's on me."

Jimmy the Ice Man, whose impoverished people have suffered for centuries at the hands of one oppressor or another, has taken pity on my small salary.

He insists, pressing the soda gently into my hands.

LOSING IT

TRAVIS AND RIVERS found this lost kitten in the shrine. They decided it might be cool to torment it. Capture it. Swing it around by the scruff of its neck like some stuffed animal. They saw that their actions upset me. And so they decided to kill the kitten. Nothing else to do.

"Hey, Kayla. What a pretty pussy, don't you think?"

"Let the damned cat go, Rivers."

"What for?" It was Rivers, the guy I didn't know too well.

"Say I won't toss this little pussy off a cliff?" That was Travis, tormenting me to relieve the boredom.

Rivers in mock astonishment: "You won't."

"Say I won't?"

Both of them playing for my benefit—which I hated. I did not want to see an innocent creature thrown to its death.

I moved to stop them, but Travis skipped out of reach.

"Hey. Say I won't smash this little pussy's head with a rock?"

"Fuck you, jackass!" I moved to stop him.

I grabbed the kitten and held it safe.

What then?

There was a local at the shrine. He had been watching us, and now I approached him.

We exchanged greetings in Arabic, and I explained things.

"Those are bad soldiers up there who want to kill this small cat. Please carry it away from here and—"

"Take it?"

"Yes, please."

"Okay."

And we exchanged farewells.

That same night Travis lost it. Matt found me to tell me just as I was getting off shift.

"He's all curled up. Like a baby. Completely freaked out. Crying and punching himself. Walking around, mumbling bullshit to himself. I try to talk to him, but he won't talk to me. Maybe you—"

"There's nothing to say, Matt. He was a total dickhead today."

"Sure," Matt said, soothingly. "Sure, I know. Yeah. That's right. But maybe you could—I don't know—just talk to him. Anything."

I went. But Travis was even worse than I imagined.

"Hey."

"Get the *fuck* away."

"Listen, if you want to talk or anything, I'll—"

"*Bitch.*"

"I just wondered if—"

Travis kept freaking out. A complete loss of control. Nothing held back. I don't know that I'd ever seen anything like this before. It was like some episode. A psychotic break. There was nothing I could do to make any difference.

I hung around for a while, just to keep an eye on him. But eventually Rivers showed up and I went back to bed.

"Hey."

"Hey."

"Back there last night with Travis," Rivers said. "That was cool. Trying to help and all. That was cool."

"He's a friend," I said. "He was having a bad night. I thought maybe I could help snap him out of it."

"Uh-huh. I tried, too. After you went to sleep. Same bad luck. The guy was unreachable. Rough night."

"Yeah."

"Listen," Rivers said, looking at me hard. "You know Travis tells me you're some kind of kinky slut."

"The fuck he does?" I blurted, my shock tinged with outrage.

Rivers studied me a moment longer.

"Nah," he said, slapping my thighs. "Nah. He never said that. I'm just bullshitting you. That's bullshit. He never said that."

I looked at him as if he was an asshole. Which maybe he was.

"Listen." Rivers was this slightly overweight guy who swaggered like a stud. No doubt covering for his own deep insecurities, I thought. Not my type. At all. "Seriously, though. I'm having this question about my girlfriend. Whether to make her my fiancée."

"Yeah?"

"Yeah."

He showed me this Polaroid. A washed-out blonde, her face a bit blurry.

"Nice," I said, politely. "Pretty."

"Yeah," he said, taking the photo back. "And I was wondering if maybe you thought that was, like, I don't know. You know." He laughed, trying to act cute.

"My opinion?" I hardly knew this guy. But I definitely did not find him cute.

"Well," he started again. "It's like this." He scratched his armpit, looking around. "Like I've had sex with sixty-eight women. And I always wanted to make it to seventy before I married. So if I marry this girl, you know, I'll never make my dream." He smiled. "Like I'd be two short."

"Yeah?"

"Yeah. I'd be two short of fucking seventy girls."

"Yeah?" I wondered why there was suddenly no one else around. And why this guy was telling me this. Though that part I could already guess.

"Well, um, it's like this." He looked at me dead-on. "Do you want to be number sixty-nine?"

I burst out laughing.

"Uh-huh, right," I said. This was too ridiculous. "Sure thing. I'll *definitely* be number sixty-nine, Rivers. Right now. Right here. Would that work for you?"

And now he was laughing too.

"Ha-ha-ha. Sure thing. Absolutely, Kayla. Let's do it in the *hajjis'* shrine."

And we were both laughing, because I was not in the least bit interested in this dude. Frankly I found it hard to imagine who would be.

Hajjis. One of the several words we routinely used to describe the Iraqi people.

The *hajj* is one of the five pillars of Islam. It refers to the pilgrimage to Mecca. Therefore, technically, a *hajji* is one who has gone on the *hajj*. But soldiers called the locals *hajjis* regardless of an Iraqi's religion or ethnicity and oblivious to whether or not this particular local had traveled to Mecca. That was completely irrelevant.

It was no different from the nasty words American soldiers have used throughout our history to describe our enemies in war. The first thing any soldier did in a combat situation was learn to dehumanize the enemy. In prior wars we called them *nips* or *chinks* or *gooks* or *krauts* or *slopes*. In Iraq we called them *hajjis*, but we also called them *sadiqis*—which means "my friends"—or *habibis*—"my darlings." (Soldiers seldom had any idea what these Arabic words meant.) We called them *towelheads. Ragheads. Camel jockeys. The fucking locals.* Words that ensured that we didn't see our enemy as people—as somebody's father or son or brother or uncle.

Later that same week this lieutenant showed up and ordered us to put up concertina wire everywhere. He discussed the possibility of booby traps and the need for all of us to dig in. Adopt fighting positions.

It made no sense at all unless the goal was to lose the hearts and minds of the people. To make them stop thinking of us as *liberators* and start thinking of us as *occupiers*.

But we unfurled the rolls of c-wire, stacking them two or three high, ripping the crap out of our gloves in the process. We began by restricting access to the Yezidi shrine. We made it so any local driving up had to zigzag through a series of c-wire barriers to get near the shrine. We continued by establishing checkpoints along the road up to our OP. To slow people down. And sometime later still, we ordered people to park their vehicles some distance away, and then walk up to the shrine.

I recognized that this sort of thing made sense from a security standpoint. It made sense because at the Tal Afar airfield there would be a mortar attack sometime later that summer. And later still, a car would be driven straight at a guard point in Tal Afar. Things like this did begin to occur later that summer in the area we were in. At this time, though, things were still good. The locals loved us. The Yezidi people adored us. You had to wonder if the subsequent souring of relations with the locals was connected to the escalation in our security. Whether when you cut people's access off to their religious shrines and began to treat them like criminals, they then maybe started to act like criminals?

At least *I* had to wonder this.

On the other hand we were extremely close to the Syrian border. And there was no reason not to think that someone might get the smart idea to attack us. We were a very weakly guarded American location. It would be the easiest thing in the world for someone to take us out. But on a gut level this fortification of our OP struck most of us as simply absurd. The fortification of our site encouraged us to hole up, and it encouraged the locals to minimize their contact with us. We moved dutifully to establish fighting positions that would block potential fire coming at us and keep the enemy from seeing us clearly.

However, we didn't have a lot of materials to make our fighting positions. We had rocks. Lots and lots of rocks. That was it. So our fighting positions involved piling rocks into a kind of enclosure where we might comfortably take cover.

The locals, who built their homes and their walls and everything else by stacking rocks on top of one another, saw us in our little rock-piling project.

They watched us, intrigued.

"No, no. Please. Let us help you."

"This is a military precaution," we explained. "To protect us. From attack."

"Yes. Yes. But please. Let us assist. We know how to do this *better.*"

So we agreed. What else were we going to do? And so the locals built our fighting positions for us.

To help us protect ourselves. From them.

In late July I was lucky enough to be allowed to visit Zoe at her site in Mosul, at 2nd Brigade's BSA (brigade support area), for a few days of R & R. They lived in buildings there, with indoor toilets and running water. There was a pizza place available, and a store with ice cream and other snacks. It was great to get to spend some time with my friend and a few days off work.

While I was there, we learned that Saddam Hussein's two sons—Uday and Qusay—had been killed by Special Forces in Mosul.

The Army moved quickly to establish roadblocks throughout the city. Locals were picked up in sweeps for interrogations on any and all kinds of charges. Maybe they were carrying a pistol— even though in Iraq *every* man carried a weapon almost all the time. Maybe they were carrying more money than a soldier thought they should. Basically any guy we wanted to pick up for questioning was picked up for questioning. Some of the detainees were brought to the BSA and thrown in a pen.

There was a sudden need for anyone fluent in Arabic. So I

was asked: "Will you assist in prescreening?" This was my time off. My first real time off in six months, but I volunteered to do Human Intelligence (HUMINT). Not my job. Not my responsibility. But of course I agreed to help.

I was asked to collect basic file information on people. Name. Date of birth. Occupation. Real straightforward stuff. We knew—and the detainees knew that we knew—that no one there had Intel value. No one had anything to do with Uday or Qusay. Just ordinary locals unlucky to be at the wrong place at the wrong time. They knew they were all going to get released by the end of the night. Which was what happened. Everyone got released.

But the job demanded that we treat everyone the same. That we treat everyone suspiciously—as possibly the one asshole here who *did* support terrorism or whatever. Until we knew who they were, we assumed this guy might be the bad guy. We didn't start from a position of presuming innocence. Quite the opposite. That was the routine, and we followed it.

So this one guy came in, drunk and disorderly.

"What is your name?" I asked in Arabic.

No answer.

"Do you speak English?" I asked again in Arabic.

He shook his head.

A few minutes later he started to curse me in English.

"Why did you lie when you said you spoke no English?" I asked in English.

He shrugged and smiled. He knew exactly what I was saying, and I was getting pissed off.

All the other detainees were moving through the process, answering our questions, and heading back out onto the streets of Mosul. But as the evening went on, this one guy was not going anywhere. Periodically he cursed us out in either Arabic or English, announcing that he had no plans to cooperate with anyone. So it was a question: What were we going to do with him?

"Listen." I attempted a good-cop routine at some point, seeing if it might make this problem go away. "Would you like a cigarette?"

I held a cigarette out to him. I wanted nothing more than to get this guy to cooperate so we could release him. Get him off our hands.

"No, no," he said, drunkenly distressed. "I have my own cigarettes." And he jutted his chin down toward his shirt pocket on his right side. "Just there."

His hands were zip-tied behind his back. He was requesting that I reach into his pockets for him.

I began to get angry again, and he saw this.

"My cigarettes," he said, sneering at me. Goading me. "Mine are *good* cigarettes."

Then I lost it.

"*Fuck* you!" I said. "I'm trying to be nice by offering you a cigarette. But if you don't want my cigarette, you can screw yourself. You won't have any cigarette."

I put my cigarette in my mouth. And I smoked it.

He whined for almost an hour. At some point I felt like whacking his damned skull—anything to make him shut up.

I found myself yelling. I found myself calling this jerk every insulting name I knew. It was just me and this one other soldier, and he was yelling at the guy, too. It was making me even angrier that the guy knew we couldn't touch him—or he was so drunk that he didn't care if we did.

I don't even want to repeat what I said; it sickens me now to think about it.

I grabbed a broom handle and banged it loud on some pipe attached to the wall.

"Rise and fucking shine, you asshole!"

Yet yelling at this guy did also feel perversely good. Because it was not something I was allowed to do. No one does this in our society; we don't just decide we can *scream* at random people who have their hands tied and who have no power to resist.

I don't like to admit it, but I enjoyed having power over this guy.

He was drunk, and at some point all he wanted was to sleep. His energy burned away and there was nothing left. He nodded off.

Sleep deprivation is an accepted and widely used tactic in these situations. Especially in a room where you have complete control over the environment.

I was not going to let this fucking guy fall asleep. He was unhappy about this, and he let us hear about it. But his obvious weariness fueled my pleasure in making him unhappy.

I was uncomfortable with these feelings of pleasure at his discomfort, but I still had them. It did occur to me that I was seeing a part of myself I would never have seen otherwise.

Not a good part.

For months afterward, I think about this episode, minor though it really was. I wonder if my own creepy sense of pleasure at my power over this man had anything to do with being a woman in this situation—the rarity of that enormous power over the fate of another human being. But maybe it has nothing to do with being female. I've talked to a number of people—both guys and girls—who did these sorts of interrogations of detainees for months. People who relished their sense of power. They *loved* doing this job, though I've come to wonder what it must be like (maybe especially for a guy) to come back from doing this work for six months and live again with a wife and a small child. What kind of readjustment is that? What kind of psychological damage does this kind of work do? How long does it take to recover from a situation where he gets used to being suspicious of everyone and where he uses threats and intimidation to get what he wants? And then comes home to a wife and a three-year-old?

All of us, guys and girls, were in a situation in Iraq where we were powerless much of the time. Powerless to change what we did. Powerless to go home. Powerless to make any real decisions about how we were living our lives while deployed. And then we found ourselves in this situation where we had all this power over another person.

And suddenly we could do whatever the fuck we wanted to them.

Returning to the mountain site after those few days in Mosul, I get off shift one night in the middle of the night. It's maybe two in the morning, and I'm not at all sleepy yet. So I head over to the COLT OP to visit with Matt. I know what times their shifts are supposed to be running, and I know that Matt comes on shift right around now. I figure we can hang out until I'm ready to crash.

It's dark, not pitch black, but really dark. So I have to get in close before I can see who it is.

"Hey, where's Matt?"

It's Rivers.

"Oh," he smiles. "I didn't wake him up for his shift."

I'm looking around. "That's weird, huh?"

"No problem," he says. "It's no problem."

I'm thinking I'm not going to let Rivers run me off. And being a girl, I'm also not going to be rude and leave. *Okay, 'bye! I wasn't here to see you anyway!*

"Yeah," I say hesitantly. "It's no problem."

So I stand there awkwardly. Rivers and I make small talk.

Things happen fast after that.

It's dark, but not so dark that I can't decipher at some point that Rivers's pants are open. That he's got one hand on his penis. And then suddenly, he's also got one hand on my arm.

He's pulling me pretty firmly toward him, maneuvering my hand toward his crotch.

"What the *fuck*—"

I pull back hard, but Rivers is strong. He's still grabbing my arm, preventing me from leaving.

"*No*," I say. "No, no, no, no, no. Let me go. *Let me the fuck go.*"

"What?" He is genuinely puzzled sounding. "Nobody has to know. We don't have to tell *anybody*."

"Dude," I'm saying as calmly as I can, while still trying to wrest my arm free of him. "I'm *not* interested. I don't want to do this."

And my mind is spinning, seeking some angle that might throw this guy off.

"Dude, what about your girlfriend? Your fiancée? You know, she's a real pretty girl. I mean, shouldn't you be thinking about her?"

"She doesn't matter. And besides, nobody would know."

So I am getting upset. I know I'm tougher now than I was

when I was thirteen, and I do have my *weapon*—but this is *intimidating*. To have this guy physically restraining me. At least on some level, I know I can yell, and Matt would probably wake up. But still . . .

The *shame* of being in a position where you might have to do that. Yell for help. Like some damn damsel in distress. Knowing that you would have to explain what just happened here.

But eventually Rivers drops his grip on my arm. He lets me go.

I leave and head back to my vehicle.

I go to sleep that night, thinking: I am going to have to report this.

The next morning I'm writing in my journal about the incident with Rivers when he appears.

"Listen, Kayla," he says, all sheepish. Looking anywhere but at me. "I apologize. I was totally out of line back there. I hope there are no hard feelings. It was dumb, and it was wrong. So I hope you can, you know, accept my apology on this."

And just like that, he's gone again.

This throws me even more. I have all this righteous anger built up. And—*wham!* An apology? It feels like cheating. Like: This guy steps *way* over the line, and now he gets to be able to have it all just go away. Because now he's *sorry?*

But I'm thinking: He did apologize. Maybe he understood. Maybe he gets it. So I do not bring up the Rivers incident with anyone right away.

For one thing I have to assume that if it comes right down to it, the guys would all back him. As somebody on their team, in their unit, in their MOS.

One of the boys.

If I am to force this issue—if I am to ask them to be loyal to Rivers or be loyal to me—what might happen? I have to imagine which way that would go. This sucks.

As much as the Army would like to tell us that it's not true, girls who file EO (equal opportunity) complaints are treated badly. Even if your chain of command encourages females to file sexual harassment claims—to stand up about these kinds of incidents—in reality, they are discouraged. Technically, if you read the EO regulations, you can file an EO complaint in the Army if you are offended by just about anything. Like somebody telling a dirty joke. If it offends you, you can file a complaint about it.

Needless to say guys do not like girls who file EO complaints. They will talk shit about them. They will not want to be around them more than is absolutely necessary.

Even *girls* don't like girls who file EO complaints—they don't want to rock the boat. Girls don't want to be perceived as filing a frivolous complaint. There's still the assumption that girls lie about harassment to get what they want—to advance their careers or to punish somebody they dislike.

So it's very risky. You don't want to be perceived as overreacting.

But what Rivers did was not like telling a dirty joke. I can and will put up with a lot. I *do* put up with a lot. I am very understanding about a lot of male behavior. I know these guys are under tremendous pressure. They are in a rough environment. They are away from their lover, their family, and everything they know—for a long time. So am I, and I know it isn't easy on any of us. And I don't want to pursue an investigation and risk ruining someone's career under these circumstances. Plus, to be honest, I am afraid that if I do file a complaint, Rivers would tell on me for drinking alcohol. Turn it around. Get me in trouble if I get him in trouble.

You hear all kinds of stories. I hear this one story about some girls in the Navy who came forward about being raped. Then *they* got into trouble because they were drinking when it happened. And they were underage. And so they're the ones who ended up getting punished. Though this only came out because they had come forward about being sexually assaulted. Which is the bigger crime? But that's what happened.

But the more I think about what Rivers did, the more it bothers me.

I finally speak to Staff Sergeant Kelly.

"Look. If something happens with one of the guys in your unit that I think is really inappropriate, do you think I should tell one of you about it? Like you or Sergeant First Class Jakubiak?"

"Yes," Kelly says. He doesn't push me to explain. "You should definitely talk to someone about it."

At this point I still have no idea how this would be handled. I have no idea whether this is something their unit is going to take seriously. But I do soon afterward speak with SFC Jakubiak and explain what happened. I ask that none of this be considered a formal complaint. There is an entire system in the Army set up to file formal complaints. There are military personnel whose job is to handle complaints like this. But I do not want to ruin this guy's career over what I imagine may be an isolated incident in his life.

So I leave the matter for his unit to handle internally. To talk to him or deal with him as they see fit, but for me not to go on record.

And Rivers is pulled off the mountain sometime after this.

Reassigned. I do not know whether there is any connection to what I said or not.

So I feel somewhat good about this, but also not so good at the same time. When you decide to allow people to handle things informally, you never know the result. You don't see somebody get demoted. You don't know if someone yells at him. You don't know if he gets talked to. You don't know if anything is done at all. That's what you give up when you decide to trust somebody else to handle things informally.

The story didn't end there, however. Not exactly.

At a later point, possibly a month after Rivers was reassigned, some other fire support guy I'd never met before came up to the mountain for a brief period of time. He was filling a slot while someone else in the unit was on leave. This guy let me know pretty fast that he was friends with Rivers.

Soon enough he found me so we could have a little chat.

"Hey," he said, all fake smiles. "Let me ask you about something."

And I was thinking, This is about Travis or something like that. His bad night. The breakdown and so forth. I don't know why this is what I thought, but I did.

"No, that's not going to happen," I said. "I don't want to talk about it."

"Come on, now. Don't be shy."

"Look. I don't know you. And I don't really want to talk about anything with you."

But he hounded me a little.

"No," he said. "I *really* have to ask you this."

So I stopped and turned back to listen.

"What?"

He just launched in.

"Rivers tells me that you came over here in the middle of the night one night. He says you said: 'Oh, please let me suck your dick. I want to suck your dick so bad.' And that he said: 'Oh, no. I have a girlfriend, and I love her so much.' And that you said: 'Oh, that's so sad 'cause I want to suck your dick so bad.' And he said: 'No, no. We can't.' And that you were *very* disappointed. *Very* upset."

I wanted to kill the motherfucker for talking shit about me like this. I wanted to kill him because I let him off without a complaint.

It felt like such a betrayal. It makes no sense, I know, but I felt like the COLT guys let me down. Like somehow they were *all* responsible. I had trouble dealing with them for a long while after that.

Everything shifted sometime that August, like water once simmering coming to a boil. You could feel the heat in everyone's mood. We were not in this together any longer. Nasty down the mountain, the insurgency gathered strength day by day. Ugly up here, too.

Like the day some of the guys—tossing a football—told rape jokes. (Are there any jokes about rape that are funny?) My blood—how else to put this?—"froze."

I collapsed. Went into a downward spin. Out of control. Felt the bottom and pushed past it.

After Rivers's friend confronted me, and I withdrew from the COLT guys, things got a little freaky for me. I began to lose it.

I began to experience intrusive images. They were like snapshots. Sudden and disturbing shots of Baghdad on patrol in the spring with Delta Company. The man in pain, bleeding to death in front of me. Or sometimes they were movie clips. A short film in which I watched myself watch him die. And I'm helpless to save him. Utterly powerless to make a difference here. I watch the flies hover. The blood on his legs. The medic. Me running. Attempting to calm the crowd. Like I said, these could be short films, but mainly they were snapshots. A lot of intrusive snapshots.

They happened day or night. And they became difficult for me. I didn't know what it meant. And it was doubly hard because I don't usually have visual memories. My usual memories are stories or words. Not pictures. So these images hit me harder than they might have otherwise. I couldn't make them go away. They didn't come when I was sleeping. When I slept I didn't dream. It was during my waking life that these images intruded.

Did the Rivers incident set this off? Or Rivers's friend? Or that we finally learned that our deployment was going to last a full year? (They kept announcing extensions to our tour—June, then July, then September, until they finally told us it would be March; by that point the news was anticlimactic.)

What was it? Was it my weight loss? I was no longer losing weight, but I was not gaining it back, either. Even with the help of all the Yezidi vegetables, I'd only been able to stabilize my weight.

Was it the guys?

One afternoon Matt approached me.

"What's the deal with you, Williams? You always want to be the center of attention." He was not joking with me now. He was angry. "And by the way, I think you're a whore."

Flipped out on me out of nowhere. And I decided I couldn't

be friends with him because he sulked and pouted and acted hateful because I wouldn't fuck him.

Later that same day Matt apologized.

"About earlier? I'm really sorry about that. I didn't mean it. That was totally wrong of me. I know you're really sensitive about that."

And later still, soon after Matt got moved down from the mountain, he had his own breakdown. Lost it and got really bad. Let himself go. Quit cutting his hair and got all twitchy; talked about how he'd been beating locals at checkpoints. Lost it so bad people got worried enough to think about command referring him for mental health.

But the guys losing it made some kind of sense. Take Matt or Travis. Both of them enlisted at eighteen right out of high school. After their AIT, they went to Korea for a year. Then back to Fort Campbell for a month, and then to Afghanistan for another six months. Then back to the States for six months— interrupted by a one-month rotation at JRTC (joint readiness training center)—and then Iraq for another year. At some point we calculated that both of them had been in the Army for thirty-seven months—Matt was still only twenty-one—and in that time they'd been away from home for thirty-two months. That's intense pressure for anyone to handle.

Me? What's my excuse? I watched some guy die once. Still felt guilt about it. Like I contributed to his death.

And now the guys I considered my friends were treating me like a *girl*. I was tits, a piece of ass, a bitch or a slut or whatever, but never really a *person*.

Bros before hos.

My appetite vanished despite the weight loss. I cried every

day, and felt like I couldn't handle it anymore. The shit was too overwhelming. Everything was. No one asked or cared—or even *noticed*—what the fuck I felt. I withdrew even more. Felt increasingly lethargic. Didn't want to go for hikes. Just wanted to lie down. Read. Sleep. And I felt this powerful desire to be even thinner and thinner. Until I could simply slip away. Disappear.

Eat less and less and less . . .

It was around this time that I contemplated offing myself. It could all be over in a moment. It would be too easy.

UNCEREMONIOUS

FINALLY BACK FROM pulling mission in the mountains, I am feeling useless. That's when there's an awards ceremony at Tal Afar. What's the point of an awards ceremony? It's almost as ridiculous as the mandatory safety briefs we undergo: Is it really important to learn over and over again the hazards of handling fuel? And what good are suicide-prevention courses?

Here we are in Iraq getting pulled from mission every three months to receive a suicide-prevention brief.

"Suicide is a widespread and common problem," the instructor will say. "It is not a sign of weakness. It does not mean that you are a bad person if you are having suicidal thoughts. Sometimes it's a desperate cry for help. Sometimes it's a chemical problem. Sometimes you may notice somebody you know who has been very depressed suddenly get better. But you should remain concerned because that's often when people *do* commit suicide. So it is very important for us to review with you today the warning signs of suicide.

"What are some of the things that you should be looking for and if you see them are potential warning signs for suicide? What are some of the triggers that might lead somebody to consider suicide? Let's review these. Anyone?"

We suck it up, and people start reciting the answers by rote:

"Somebody who starts to give away their possessions."

"Somebody who starts talking about things being over for them."

"Somebody who starts talking about how they can't see any other solution."

"Somebody who talks about having significant family problems."

"Somebody who talks about having serious financial problems."

"Somebody who has just been in trouble or punished by his chain of command."

We watch Army videos during these suicide-prevention briefs.

The videos depict soldiers acting out the warning signs for suicide.

"My father and mother are breaking up. Divorcing. And I can't handle it. I can't stand that there's nothing I can do. I'm feeling so helpless." And so on.

A title tells us that this actor/soldier subsequently kills himself.

Another actor/soldier appears on the screen.

"I never saw it coming. I never imagined that John was so depressed."

An authoritative voice-over cuts in.

"But he should have seen it coming! Notice how John gave away his stereo! And he was clearly collecting pills! He no longer socialized with friends! Friends who should have taken preventive steps to save John—before it was too late!"

Video over, the instructor flips on the lights.

"If you suspect that someone you know is suicidal, you need to immediately report that person to your chain of command or the chaplain or a mental health personnel. You need to be more concerned about saving their life than saving their pride. You must address this problem. Every one of us must be aware. Everybody must pay attention. It's a tremendous problem."

Easy to say. Harder to do. There is a huge stigma in the military about this topic. We are supposed to be tough. We are supposed to be strong. We are never supposed to exhibit weakness. And suicide is definitely seen as taking the easy way out. It is definitely perceived as a weak response to a difficult situation. (I learned much later that the suicide rate for American soldiers in Iraq in 2003 was unusually high—close to double the Army's rate of 11.1 for each one hundred thousand soldiers in 2002.)

We also receive other quarterly safety briefs. For instance there's the brief on proper methods for handling fuel. (We must wear gloves. We should wear goggles. Be sure to wear the correct safety equipment. And so forth.) And the safe way to handle a generator. There's also the position on sexual harassment or POSH, which we also review on the same days as the safety briefs. We review the two general types of sexual harassment. These are "quid pro quo" and "hostile work environment."

"What does 'quid pro quo' mean? What are the various types of sexual harassment? There's verbal and nonverbal harassment. There's physical harassment. There's threatening somebody with punishment if they don't do what you want sexually. There's rewarding somebody if they do what you want sexually. You have to be really careful and consider everyone's feelings no matter what you're doing. Even putting up posters of girls might offend somebody. If I tell you a dirty joke, and there's somebody sitting over there, and they get offended, I'm wrong for telling that joke."

We also review the reasonable person clause. This means that for something to be sexual harassment, it must be something a reasonable person would consider inappropriate behavior. (None of us ever have any idea who this reasonable person is.)

We review equal opportunity training. ("What is racism? What is sexism? What is racial prejudice? What do these things mean? And how do you see them in your daily lives?") It gets a little bizarre. Imagine a roomful of mainly eighteen- to twenty-two-year-old boys responding to these questions.

"Could someone please give me an example of verbal sexual harassment?"

The instructor is fucking asking for it.

Of course the guys immediately start yelling things out.

My own position is that if there were *real* concern for our safety, they'd get us the hell out of this combat zone. *That* would promote safety. But the Army doesn't think that way. If it thinks at all.

I respected and understood the need for safety briefs. But at some slightly later time, the Army also began to institute various "ethnic themes" for our chow halls in Iraq. For instance, there were displays about Hispanic heritage and African American heritage, and on those days we ate foods from those minority backgrounds: collard greens or fried chicken for African American heritage and fajitas or burritos for Mexican American heritage. Basically, I respected and understood the rationale for these gestures as well. But it also convinced me it was absolutely time for us to go home.

I'm sorry, and I don't mean to sound rude, but if the Army could take time out in Iraq to serve up fried rice to celebrate

Asian American heritage, then it was definitely time for them to send my ass home.

The awards ceremony should have been a thrill. Standing in formation listening to a little speech from our battalion commander about our contribution to the war effort. Getting a medal pinned on. Photographs. Applause. An ARCOM (Army commendation medal) for my service. It should have been great. It should have been exciting.

But it wasn't. I felt pissed off.

My promotion was still fucked up, and it didn't appear that anyone was working to resolve the issue.

And we all noticed in the ceremony that everyone who was a staff sergeant or above was getting a higher honor, the Bronze Star, no matter what they had done. This medal was supposed to be a big deal, but it was looking more political. Some squad leaders put their soldiers in for this medal, while mine did not. Staff Sergeant Moss put me in for the same ARCOM as Lauren, even though Lauren never went out on combat patrol. Meanwhile, people I knew who were never in harm's way—and never led any soldiers—were getting a Bronze Star. It was insulting.

At the same time I am very hesitant to mention this at all because I do not believe that I deserved the honor of a Bronze Star. But neither did I believe that these people deserved it. Awards carelessly given lose their meaning.

To make matters worse, the only two people of my rank who did get Bronze Stars were getting them for doing the identical work I did in Baghdad—going out with the infantry. And they had bulletproof plates in their flak vests.

I mentioned this casually to my new platoon leader, now that

LT Malley had moved up to XO. She told me that those two guys "went above and beyond the linguist job."

Again my head filled with images of a bloodied and screaming man. But I said nothing. She wasn't with us in Baghdad. She had no idea what I did or saw.

Still, the insult of her careless words rankled, and my frustration deepened.

Later that same day, after the ceremony, I cornered our platoon sergeant.

"Look," I said, "it's not about the damn medal. I don't care about the medal."

"You seem upset," he said.

"Upset? If what I did wasn't 'above and beyond,' why should I be receiving an ARCOM? Why should I be receiving anything at all? In fact, you can have the medal. I don't want the ARCOM. And my promotion—I don't want that either. You can shove them both—"

"Calm down," he said. But I'd gotten his attention. "What's going on?"

He was one of those men who didn't notice a complaint until you threw a fit. Then he took notice. But it felt awful that I had to have a temper tantrum to get his attention. I explained the whole situation.

"Listen, we're working on your promotion. I'll see what I can do."

Whatever. (For the record, more than a year later, it still had not been resolved.)

I didn't know Specialist Berenger from a hole in the ground. Never knew her at DLI, where she studied Arabic, too. We were there at different times. Never knew her in-country, either—she had only just arrived about three weeks before. This civilian linguist came to me to ask me a question.

"You know Specialist Berenger?" he asked.

"Can't say that I do."

"She's having some family problems."

"Yeah," I said, chuckling. "Who hasn't? Where I come from, having family problems is the universal sign for human."

"No. I mean, yeah," he stuttered. "Sure." He cleared his throat. "I'm just saying if you find a moment, maybe you could speak to her. Draw her out. Talk to her a little. Find out what's wrong, maybe."

I never asked him why he was asking *me*. Did I look like a camp counselor for troubled teens? I didn't agree to do it. I didn't disagree. To be honest, I didn't think about it one way or the other.

Until I saw her, that is. In the tent. As it happened, we were alone for the moment.

She was not as young as I expected. Or as crazy. In fact, I couldn't for the life of me figure out what the civilian linguist was all worked up about. Was she depressed? Who wasn't? Seemed to me a rational response to an irrational situation.

But she was fidgety. I hate it when girls twirl their hair in their fingers, round and round. Nervous habits make *me* nervous.

I introduced myself. She introduced herself.

We engaged in small talk. She was HUMINT. I'm SIGINT (Signal Intelligence). But we'd had some of the same teachers back in Monterey, and we talked about them for a few minutes. She was a little shy, maybe. A little reserved. But I was thinking about what the civilian linguist said, and so I pursued it.

"My family," I said more or less out of nowhere. "My family is nuts. Just nuts. My mom thinks I'm on vacation here. Sometimes I'm not sure she understands that this is a war. She writes me and asks whether I'm going to get a chance to see the Pyramids. I'm like: Mom, the Pyramids are in Egypt. I'm in Iraq. You know— land of the evil dictator. Weapons of mass destruction. Iraq. I-R-A-Q. *Iraq*. Remember? And she writes me back hoping I'll be safe, and asking me how's the food. Am I eating okay and should she send chocolates. Chocolates? Can you believe it?"

Berenger fiddled with her hair.

"My folks don't know I'm here."

I stopped at that.

"How can that be?" I asked.

"I never told them I deployed. I never told them because I wasn't sure they wanted to know." She paused. "We don't talk too often."

"Damn," I said. "That's rough. Maybe you could send them a note. An e-mail. Put yourselves back in touch. That might be a good thing." Pause. "Under the circumstances and all."

'Yeah," she said, not sounding too convinced. "It's not a good situation, you know?"

"Sure." But I had no idea what she meant. And I didn't know if I should be asking, either.

"Listen," I said. "Families are tough. But they're family. I mean, you might want to let your folks know what's up. That you're here."

Berenger looked at me a moment.

"You know what you said about your mom? That's so incredible, you know? Because I never would have guessed it."

"Why's that?"

"Because you seem so totally together. I wouldn't imagine you had problems."

I looked at her real close for any indication Berenger was mocking me. But no. Not a shred of that. She meant it. Now that's *scary*.

"Yeah," I said. "Sure. But sometimes things aren't exactly what they seem. You know?"

She smiled a sad smile.

"Roger that," she said, noncommittal.

Right then some guys noisily descended on the tent, throwing things onto their cots, acting all loud and disruptive.

"Hey," I said to Berenger. "I go out on mission again tomorrow, but when I get back—"

"Sure, me too," she said. "I head out soon also."

"Let's talk again. I mean, *anytime*. Maybe get some chow together. How's that sound?"

"Sure. That would be good."

It was awkward, but it felt okay. It felt fine. I rummaged through my brain and thought back to the guy who said *talk to her*. Okay, done. And if she wanted more, I'd announced that I could be there for her. What more could I do?

That was it, I guess.

Four days later Berenger was dead. Suicide. A single self-inflicted gunshot wound to the head. That's all it took. I don't know more than that, a suicide not being the sort of thing people wanted to discuss in detail. (This was still more than her family ever learned about the circumstances surrounding her death. When the Army informed Berenger's parents that their daughter was dead, they never asked how it happened. They never asked how she died. And so the Army never told them.)

I did not see this coming. And I wondered: What the fuck is wrong with this place? And thought: What's my problem that I did not see this coming? Should I have done more?

However, that's not the part of the story that gets me every time I think about it now.

So Berenger's dead. And the company organizes a memorial service.

No, let me rephrase that. The company *orders* all soldiers to attend a memorial service.

Actually, let me rephrase that one more time. We are told we have a choice. Attend the memorial service for Berenger or explain to the battalion commander why we don't want to go. No one really wants to attend the memorial service—we didn't really know her and it is depressingly morbid. But we do it. Typical Army. A choice that's no choice at all.

Basically, though we can't say it, we're pissed at Berenger. What gives her the right to do what she did? She's here less than a month—and *pow*. She offs herself. We've been here—most of us— six months or more. Suffered and felt so damned awful for days and weeks at a time, of course we may have considered it. But we didn't do it. And here she comes in, and she gets a little down— and pulls the trigger. And that's the end of that. Why the hell is she getting *recognition* for this? There's a war on. Don't we have any-thing better to do than memorialize a girl who couldn't take it?

But we do it. We attend. Sitting on folding chairs under the blazing sun in the dust.

A chaplain speaks.

Her platoon sergeant speaks. The first sergeant speaks. The commander speaks.

A girl reads a Bible quote.

By the time our battalion commander stands to speak, this is getting old real fast. It's hot, and we're tired of sitting in the sun listening to a lot of blah-blah-blah about some poor girl no one really knew.

Of course, I'm feeling responsible. Guilty. Berenger saying that I seemed so together should have been my cue. I should have done more. I should have noticed something. Why else put us through all these suicide-prevention briefs? What's the point? I should have forced a conversation. I should have asked a question or two more. Gotten her talking about her shit. Talked to the chain of command or something.

So the BC gets up to speak.

"Specialist Berenger was a good soldier, a good person, and a good friend. She will be missed. We take these moments today to honor her and to mourn her. We recognize the sacrifice she made and the pain she must have felt. We take this time today . . ."

I'm blanking by this point. Wondering when I'll get back out on mission and away from this bullshit. From this place where words matter more than actions. But then the BC cuts off and begins again.

"I would also like to say a few more personal words about what has happened here."

She pauses, and I'm thinking *okay, here we go*. This BC lacks *tact*, this I know from experience. (Like when Lauren returns to Fort Campbell, her husband still grievously ill, the BC blurts out, "Oh, is your husband dead?" That sort of thing.) A good-enough soldier, a decent leader (for the most part). But like I said, she is seriously deficient in tact.

She says: "When I first heard about Specialist Berenger's

death, I was shocked and saddened. But as time passed, I felt another emotion. I was angry. I'm angry at Berenger. She caused this because she never reached out for help. She never went to her chain of command, never went to the chaplain. This is her fault. It should not have come to this."

The memorial service is over. We are stunned. Our disgust at Berenger's action pushed aside by our disgust at our BC. Of course I understood the BC's point. I just think a memorial service is the wrong damn time to say it. It's something you put out to your commanders so they can disseminate it down. If you have a friend that dies of HIV, you may say to other people you know and care about that this should remind everyone to use condoms. But you don't get up at her fucking memorial service and say: "Oh, she brought this on herself by not using condoms." It's tacky. And heartless.

A few days after this, I was working on my Humvee. Checking it and getting it ready to go out again on mission. I was under the hood when I heard a Humvee stop suddenly.

"Specialist Williams!"

I looked up. It was a couple of the guys from Delta Company 1/187, the guys I went with on missions in Baghdad. The man in the passenger seat jumped out and rushed over.

"This is not the proper way to do this. I know that."

I wiped engine grease from my hands. Feeling distracted and sweaty, but glad nonetheless to see these guys.

"The proper way to do what?" I asked.

"We've been looking for you everywhere. In Baghdad. In the mountains. But you're a tough one to catch."

"They keep me busy."

"Yeah, I see that. Listen," their first sergeant said. "I know this is not the proper way to do it. But we wanted you to have this." He held out a recognizable green folder, the kind that holds Army awards. "In recognition of your work with us back in the spring. For service above and beyond. You really deserve it."

It was an Army commendation medal. Just like the one I received from my own unit. But completely different. This one *counted*. It was from the infantry, and they almost never recognize support elements.

I was so touched, felt so proud.

"Thanks—"

"Listen, we're on our way out on mission. Gotta go."

I stood there, grease on my face, feeling better than I had in months.

"Good job, Specialist," he said. And they were gone in a cloud of dust.

LOCKED AND LOADED

W E HEAR ALL the time there's this expecta-
tion that as soldiers we should be willing to make sacrifices for
our jobs. Put mission first. Even if this means putting the mission
above our own personal well-being. But that's what we do. It's
what most of us believe we should do.

I could have been medevaced (medically evacuated) to
Germany for the foot surgery I needed. I told the doctors that if
I did this, I wanted a guarantee I would be sent back to Iraq to
finish my tour. But I was told that if I went to Germany, in fact,
they would fly me back to the States for surgery. More than likely
this would have meant I would not return to Iraq. So I again post-
poned my surgery, believing that whenever I decided to have it,
my tour would end. I'd get sent home. And I was not comfortable
with this.

My friends thought I was nuts. People were *trying* to get out.
To go home. *I* wanted to go home.

There are certainly lots of ways to fake it. Say you're a homo-
sexual, for instance. That would work—but it's more likely to
work if you're a guy because there's a double standard. On paper
the rules on homosexuals in the military are written the same.

But in reality most men in the Army—like most men in U.S. society—think that girl-on-girl action is hot, while dudes getting it on is filthy and disgusting. Army guys generally think lesbians rock, since clearly these are chicks just waiting for the right man to come along. What would my first sergeant do if he came across me and another girl getting it on? He'd want pictures. He'd want to join in. He'd want me and this other girl to double-team him right then and there. On the other hand, since most heterosexual men are homophobic and sexist, most straight guys figure gay men will treat them the way they themselves treat women—that is, like sex objects. And this freaks them the fuck out.

What this all means in practical terms is that females are less likely to be chaptered out (that is, forced out) of the Army for being gay than are guys. That's just the way it is.

In any case I had no desire to fake anything. Lauren and I had joked about it all the time while she was still there—we'd finish their war, but when we were done, we'd take some crazy photos and get out. But it was only a joke—in reality, we were both very dedicated. So I fought to stay in Iraq. Morally I believed that staying was the right thing to do.

What was my argument? For one thing, we simply never had enough Arabic linguists in-country as it was. We were constantly low on experienced personnel. We'd already lost a lot of people whose ETS (end term of service—that is, the date they were due to leave the service) had passed after the Army's stop-loss kept them in an entire extra year. When that final stop-loss date approached, the Army had to send them home so that they would get out on time. So these people were all leaving. Also, people could now have a PCS (permanent change of station)—that is, move to another duty station. So we were losing people to

ETS and PCS, and a few random people for other reasons—medical issues, family emergencies, pregnancies, whatever.

I felt strongly that it would be wrong for me to leave. There were people getting killed and people getting seriously injured—people with *real* problems. I didn't feel comfortable getting out of my commitment for what was a relatively minor concern. I would have to be a real jackass to leave my mission because of my foot. I also had developed a deep commitment to my fellow soldiers. My brothers in arms, or whatever cheesy way you want to say it. But it was really true. I wanted to be there for the people I'd served with this whole time.

So instead of surgery, I got the cortisone shots to deal with the pain. It was actually easier to get the shots in Iraq than it had been in America. In the States it was tough to get an appointment. The waiting period could take weeks. In Iraq I headed down to any aid station, explained what was going on, and they gave me a shot right away. It was great, except I ended up getting seven or eight cortisone shots in eight months. Doctors don't recommend more than three shots in a year. But I had to do this just so I could get by.

Finally, however, in late October, I was able to find a doctor who was willing to do the surgery in-country. So I had the surgery. In a tent at D-Rear in Mosul.

This was right around Halloween. As I came out of general anesthetic, I saw cardboard witches and goblins hanging and floating around on strings in the tent. It was a little weird.

Afterward I found out I was going to have problems with my foot for the rest of my life.

Not because of the surgery. The surgery was perfect. It was all the cortisone shots. They'd caused a permanent degradation of the fatty tissue on the ball of my foot. The two toes next to my big toe were going to be numb forever. It was a small thing, I guess, but I would never wear high heels again.

I could deal with it. What was tough was that I was not getting support from the people at D-Rear. Everyone watched me hobble around on crutches, but no one offered to help me. They were total pricks about it. No one even brought me food or water.

So I called my unit at the airfield and asked them to pick me up and bring me back to the airfield. This meant I would travel on a convoy while I was all drugged up in the back of a Humvee over a particular stretch of road where several convoys had been ambushed. I would not have my weapon. I couldn't carry a weapon while I was on narcotics. I would not be able to respond if anything happened. I would not be able to jump and run on crutches. This was all very intimidating, but once we were on the road, the drugs knocked me out. I ended up asleep in the back like a baby for a lot of the trip.

It took close to three weeks before I could handle work again.

Ambush Alley was at the edge of Mosul, right inside the city's gates. On one side of the road there was a group of buildings; on the other side there was a cemetery. As convoys moved through, they got attacked. I don't know why ambushes occurred at this location and not some other location. But they did. Not every ambush resulted in a death. But many resulted in injuries, and sometimes the injuries were serious.

A couple of weeks earlier, a convoy traveling from Mosul to the Tal Afar airfield was hit. It was a coordinated attack—there were one or two rocket-propelled grenades plus small-arms fire and an IED (improvised explosive device) all at once. The bomb in the road involved a propane tank, so there was a lot of fire. A lot of the people who got hurt got hurt with burns. I knew two of the soldiers who were hurt. One was Staff Sergeant Lott from my unit. He received burns and minor cuts—luckily, his injuries were minor enough that he was RTD (return to duty). So he got treated and was released back to us, not medevaced or hospitalized. He earned his Purple Heart all the same (anyone injured by enemy action gets one).

Lott's equipment came back to us, and there was blood on his gear. I helped First Sergeant Duggan, an absolutely amazing leader, wash everything. One of Lott's weapons magazines had been destroyed by shrapnel. We took apart his LBV (load-bearing vest) one clip at a time, so the vest could be washed. We kept the twisted magazine for Lott—as a sort of souvenir.

Staff Sergeant Shane Kelly was the second guy injured. The platoon sergeant for the COLT platoon in the mountains. A guy I was thinking I liked, though we didn't really say much about it before he left for mid-tour leave. Two weeks home. Visiting family. Seeing his daughter. And here he had just flown back into the airport in Mosul where he caught the first convoy back to Tal Afar. Ridiculous timing. Kelly was back in the country for a matter of hours when his convoy got hit. And he was *very* seriously injured. Took shrapnel in the head. Got flown out of the country immediately. To Germany—where they didn't even know if he would survive. He flatlined four times. If this had happened in any previous war, there is no question he would have died. I learned later that soldiers in this war survived at a rate nine times higher than in any prior combat, due to individual body armor— the Kevlar and the flak vest that protected the core organs. And because more of us had been trained in Combat LifeSaver so we could do better, more immediate first aid. And also due to better battlefield technology and rapid medical evacuation.

When the ambushed convoy reached the base, I learned right away that Kelly had been hurt. Only sometime later did I learn how very badly he'd been hurt. And only sometime after that did I learn that he was going to make it. That he was going to be more or less okay.

While traveling among the locals, we always kept our rifles on safe, but whether or not they were locked and loaded could vary by convoy.

Every magazine holds thirty rounds. Thirty bullets. You put the magazine into the magazine well in the bottom of the weapon. However, at that point, the rifle is not ready to fire for two reasons. The first is that the safety is still on. But the second reason is that you don't actually have a round in the chamber. And there are two ways to address this. The first way is to lock the bolt to the rear of the weapon, load the magazine, and then let the bolt ride forward. It will then chamber a round automatically. If the bolt is in the forward position when you load the weapon, you pull the charging handle back, release it, and the bolt picks up a round and chambers the round. Our weapons must have a round in the chamber for them to fire. Different weapons operate in different ways, but our weapons—once you have a round chambered and you fire for the first time—will automatically chamber a second round. And so forth. Therefore you don't actually have to go through this process and chamber each individual round every single time you fire. But you *must* have a round in the chamber to fire that first time.

In Iraq we have three degrees of weapon status: red, yellow, and green. Green means you do not have a round chambered and you do not have your magazine in your magazine well. You do not have a magazine in the weapon at all. The weapon is completely safe. Yellow means you have a magazine in the magazine well, but you do not have a round chambered. Before you can fire the weapon the first time, you would need to chamber a round. And red means you have a round chambered. Depending on the danger of the situation, we were instructed either to keep our weapons at red, yellow, or green.

With the weapon status on red, once you have that round chambered, all you have to do is flip the switch from safe to semi and pull the trigger. Flip, squeeze. It can be extremely fast. It would take you less than a second to start firing. Whereas, if you do not have a round chambered, it would take several more seconds. You are going to have to think about the process harder, and you are not going to be as responsive.

The only time you would have your weapon on green in Iraq would be while you are at a completely secure location. So once we arrive at the Tal Afar airfield or at D-Main or D-Rear, every vehicle in the convoy stops, we get out, drop our magazines, and clear our weapons. We have to aim them at the ground and fire to verify that they're cleared. If there's a click, that's that. The weapon is proved safe. But if someone fires and it discharges accidentally at this point, that person gets in a *lot* of trouble. (An accidental discharge happens a lot more often than you might imagine.)

During actual combat operations in the spring, we are consistently at red. But after combat officially ends, sometime in May or June, and once we move into SASO (sustainment and stability operations), we move to yellow almost all the time while on convoys.

SASO is supposed to be *peacekeeping*. As part of stability and support, you are supposed to be helping people out. Keeping the peace and maintaining order. It's understood that soldiers are going to die during combat; they are *not* supposed to die during SASO. But, as we all know, there have been many more deaths during SASO in Iraq than during actual combat.

So now, by the fall of 2003, as the situation gets worse and worse, we are instructed to place our weapons back to red during convoys.

It's also around this time that we receive new instructions on the ROE (rules of engagement). Actually they have been changing constantly, and it can be difficult to keep up. Like a lot of soldiers, I carry a copy of the ROE card in my Kevlar—though I'm sure it's outdated. The threat level is now high enough, we're told, for yet another escalation. So our instructions on one particular convoy are:

"If you see a guy on the side of the road on a cell phone, point your weapon at him. And if he won't get off the phone, *you can shoot him.* He might be calling in your location to somebody else. So if you think that he is on the phone passing information about your convoy and where it's going, and you feel he's a threat, you are authorized to shoot him."

I cannot believe we're told this. I think it's insane. It's crossing a line to shoot somebody just because he's on the phone. Can you imagine a foreign power coming to the United States and deciding to drive around and shoot your neighbor because he's on his cell phone? Maybe he's out there talking because he can't get a good signal in his house.

I read in *The Zanzibar Chest,* a great book by journalist Aidan

Hartley, how United Nations peacekeeping soldiers in Rwanda and Somalia always had a gun in one hand. And a spoon in the other. Increasingly I feel the U.S. Army is finding itself in a comparable situation in Iraq.

We're here to help you! We're here to help you! Oh, and shoot you—if we feel it's necessary.

It's a terrible position for any soldier on the ground to be in. I don't know if it's a fair position, either, because you are never going to build relationships with the civilian population, or win hearts and minds, when you treat everybody as a threat. It's almost impossible to walk that line.

How to explain this dilemma? If you see someone heading toward you, he could be approaching to offer you information. He could have an explosive device strapped to his waist and be about to kill you. He might want to ask for food. You have to make that call—instantaneously. You have to decide whether or not you will allow this man anywhere near you. You have to decide whether you shoot him where he stands. Or whether you attempt to communicate with him from a distance and tell him to stop. Every car you see driving past you, you have to judge whether or not this could be an attempt to kill you. Or will the driver or passenger wave or completely ignore you? You have to make that judgment call. Every single time. Every time you see any person anywhere close to you.

In truth, every incident that happens is a completely discrete incident, but it's almost impossible to live this way. Basically we all reach a point where we have to assume that everyone is friendly (and respond accordingly), or assume that everyone is a potential enemy (and treat them as such). It simply becomes too overwhelming to play that line at every single moment. To look at each person and make that choice over and over and over again. To ask yourself: Will I give this person food? Or will I point my gun at this person? So we make one choice: We come to assume the worst about everyone. And we stick with it.

Speak to infantry soldiers who have been in tough situations for a long time, and they will say that they treat *everyone* as the enemy. That's how they deal. That's how they survive.

I consider myself a reasonably compassionate person. I speak the language, and I have Arab friends, so I believe I'm better equipped than most soldiers to see these civilians as people. Not simply as *the enemy*. But even for me there are times I am feeling overwhelmed by the situation. God, why can't we just kill everyone—or leave them to fucking kill each other? Because I cannot care any more. I cannot walk this line all the time. It's too hard. I get too angry.

Increasingly many of us are just feeling angry all the time. When we think about the local population now, we're thinking: What are you people doing? We're here to help you! And you're trying to kill us! Are you insane? Do you even *want* peace? Or freedom? Or democracy? Do you want anything? Or do you just want to kill all the time? What's wrong with you?

What is wrong with these people?

For anyone who has anything to do at either D-Main or D-Rear, the convoy leaves the airfield once a day. And then returns to the airfield sometime later that same day. Back and forth, back and forth. Commanders go to meetings. We pick up mail and supplies. People leave for R & R or mid-tour leave. The number of vehicles on any given convoy can vary dramatically. From seven to thirty or more, depending on the day.

On one particular morning I'm on a brigade convoy heading from Tal Afar to Mosul. And the local vehicles traveling with us are moving especially slowly for some reason. We routinely hire local trucks and buses to transport equipment, supplies, or people. And on this day there are quite a number of *hajji* trucks with our convoy. The *hajji* trucks are elaborately painted in colorful patterns, all tricked out with fringes on the windshields and Mercedes symbols on the front. But they are seldom in great shape. So whenever a vehicle breaks down, we have to stop and wait.

The weather is terrible. It's dark and raining, and there's a cold sharp wind that cuts through our uniforms, making everyone miserable.

So our convoy is creeping along through a section of Mosul on this awful day. And I realize that we are approaching Ambush Alley. The same section of Mosul and the same stretch of road where Kelly's convoy was attacked—and where he was seriously injured—only a few weeks before.

So I'm already tense—this road is extremely dangerous.

Did I mention the locals drive like assholes? Or like New York taxi drivers, however you want to look at it. So we're on this divided highway, with two or three lanes in one direction, and the same in the opposite direction. There's a grass divider in the middle. Even if we're driving in the left lane, the locals still like to pass us on the left by driving onto the grass. If we're in the right-hand lane, they still try and pass us on the right by driving onto the shoulder or the berm. Anytime they think we're not moving fast enough, they will attempt to pass us. Then sometimes they'll pass and cut directly in front of our vehicle.

We are all aware how locals who have cut directly in front of military vehicles have also thrown bombs back at those vehicles, or popped up from the trunk and shot at us. Therefore we are well trained never to let anyone cut us off. It is a rule never to let anyone get between your vehicle and the rest of the vehicles in the convoy.

But at the same time, in case there is a roadside bomb, you don't want your vehicle to get caught in the same blast as another vehicle. So you want to keep a certain distance between yourself and other vehicles. Each convoy commander puts out a directive about the desired interval between vehicles on his convoy. Maybe it's a ten-meter interval. Or more. Or less, depending on the convoy and location. In rural areas, a hundred meters is fine. In the city, we often traveled "nut sack to asshole" (as my first sergeant put it), that is, bumper to bumper to prevent locals from squeezing in.

The routine is this: The driver keeps his eyes on the road, looking forward and examining the road for potential roadside bombs. The passengers on the right-hand side focus their attention on their side of the vehicle. Same for the passenger behind the driver on the left-hand side. Each of us has his or her own zone, our own lane or field of fire. And that's what we are trained to focus on.

I am in the rear seat on the left side behind the driver. I don't have a door. The doors on this four-passenger Humvee have been removed. A lot of times, if a vehicle is not up-armored—that is, if it has not been fortified with armor plating and bullet-proof glass (and, at this time, very few Humvees have been up-armored)—the doors are removed to make it easier to jump in and out or to shoot. A door limits your maneuverability and your ability to move your weapon. Canvas doors would do nothing at all to protect us anyway. And they would just slow us down. So the doors are simply removed.

I'm freezing in the cold and rain and wind.

Now I'm noticing this local attempting to pass us. We're driving on the left, and this car is coming up fast on the grass beside us on the left.

It's gloomy and difficult to see, but it's clear that this car is planning to cut in ahead of us. I can tell by the way the driver is glancing back and forth that he is going to cut over.

This is making me nervous. It is also pissing me off. They should know we don't want them to do this. They should know better!

Why would anyone fuck with people who have semiautomatic weapons? Why would anyone do this?

So this vehicle is coming up on us. And coming up closer and closer.

Typically, when you're in the rear of a Humvee and a local is driving up and you don't want them to do whatever they're doing, you gesture with your weapon. Because you are always holding your weapon. Often I would have my weapon resting on my knees, and I might wave at kids with one hand while I'm holding my rifle with my other hand.

Or if I'm on convoy in the back of a cargo Humvee, and I'm looking straight out the back, and a local is moving in between vehicles in the convoy, I might gesture with my weapon at the local and then gesture to another lane. *Hey, you! Get in the other fucking lane! Don't get between us!* And they move. Believe me, they get the point. This method of silent communication with a weapon is very effective.

So I'm gesturing with my weapon at this car moving up next to us. I'm telling them: *Do not cut us off! Back off! DON'T FUCK WITH ME!*

The car is not pulling back. He is not getting the message.

It's tremendously loud with no doors. No one in the Humvee but me sees this car yet. It's my field of fire. It's my call to decide what to do next.

I raise my weapon and point directly into the car. I can feel my adrenaline pumping. I do not know what's going to happen.

I will shoot if this car is beginning to feel like a threat.

My weapon status is red. Always red on convoy now. My safety's on, though I know some soldiers are not bothering with keeping their weapons on safety anymore. But I do. It's still less than a second. Flip, squeeze. After the first round, I can fire at will.

Just then a passenger on my side turns to look for the first time.

It's a little boy. Not more than eight or nine years old. I'm pointing my weapon at a boy who looks exactly like Rick's little brother.

The boy looks at me looking at him.

I lower my rifle and hold it with one hand across my knees. Without thinking, I wave at the boy with my other hand.

And after a moment he waves back.

CROSSING A LINE

In November our team moved once again. This time it was to the large compound at 2nd Brigade's BSA (brigade support area). The compound was a lot more established than it had been in the summer, when I had first come there to visit Zoe. The cage where detainees had been held was a permanent prison now. The prisoners could stay there for a longer time. A whole infrastructure had been built up, and an entire HUMINT platoon—MI who conducted interrogations—was also stationed here now on a permanent basis.

Meanwhile the compound was also getting mortared almost daily, though nothing usually came too close. The enemy's aim was typically terrible. On one occasion, however, the mortar attack was bad—very bad. There were at least a dozen direct hits, and some were so close I heard the rocket's whistle before I heard the explosion.

You never quite got used to it. There was a bug zapper in our room. And every time a bug flew into it and got zapped, I jumped.

And yet in some ways you did get used to it. A mortar hit, and we sat there calculating the distance. *That one doesn't sound too close.*

At the same time, there were EOD teams also blowing things up at certain hours each day. So we began to joke that you'd been in-country too long if the first thing you did when you heard an explosion was look at your watch. You didn't take cover. You didn't grab Kevlar. You checked your watch. Oh, three o'clock. That's EOD. No big deal.

At some point in there, Zoe caught me up on how *her* team leader almost got *her* killed. And how pissed off she'd been about it.

Zoe's near-death experience occurred after she broke her ankle playing basketball. Her foot in a cast, she was running ops when the 2nd Brigade's BSA came under mortar fire. Getting mortared was nothing unusual, but when a blast hit fifty feet away—leaving a crater seven feet in diameter—this freaked her out. Then the radio said take cover inside. Immediately. So Zoe hobbled out of the Humvee, but her team leader appeared out of a building and stopped her.

"What are you doing? Get back in the truck and pull ops!"

He was wearing his flak vest and Kevlar. Zoe had neither.

"We're taking mortar fire!" Zoe shouted at him. "The radio said take cover!"

"No!" her team leader yelled as more mortars hit the base. "The vehicle is sufficient cover! Go back! That's an order!"

Zoe returned to the vehicle. The mortar fire continued. Then her assistant team leader rushed to the vehicle.

"Why are you still out here?" she said in panic. "It came over the radio for everyone to take cover in a building!"

Zoe responded: "Sergeant Watkins told me I had to stay here."

More mortars hit as Zoe and her assistant team leader got on the radio to headquarters. "Is a vehicle sufficient cover during this mortar attack?"

"No," the voice came back. "You *must* be inside a building."

So Zoe now called in again, this time to her platoon leadership. She said: "We are under mortar fire. And we are going to cease operations. And take cover."

"Yes!" the voice came back. "Go inside! What are you doing? Go! Go be safe!"

So Zoe and her assistant team leader shut down the system. And took cover in a building. Where they found her team leader still in his flak vest and Kevlar. *Inside the building.*

Infuriated, Zoe yelled at him. Told him she could never trust his leadership ever again. Never again trust instructions from him. Because he had not taken proper care of his soldier. Because he had chosen to put his own personal safety first. And she planned to report what had happened to her chain of command.

Which she did. To her platoon sergeant and her first sergeant. And Sergeant Watkins received his letter of reprimand. A letter that said he'd been naughty. And that was the end of it.

After I got to 2nd Brigade's BSA in November, Zoe and I were always together. We were together each day all day. When my aunt sent me cross-stitch, Zoe and I cross-stitched together. Something to do with our hands while we talked. The quietly good joy of being able to talk with somebody I loved. Someone who could talk to me about *smart* things. No more throwing rocks and talking about boobs; Zoe and I discussed issues and ideas. Religion, abortion, the death penalty, relationships, our personal development—we talked about everything. We talked about things at a level one might expect in a college classroom, a level that did not occur as often as I might have liked during my time in the military.

Zoe had turned twenty-one in Iraq. And she had grown so much in the three years I'd known her. When we'd first met, Zoe was still practically a girl. Now she was definitely a woman. Someone who had stopped believing in something simply because she'd been taught to believe it. Someone who really thought things through on her own—and believed things because she had thought long and hard about them.

When I reflect on the impact her year in Iraq had on Zoe, I am reminded of a quotation I like. The journalist E. L. Godkin said it: "The sight of a battlefield is one of the most awful lessons in international ethics which a civilized man can receive." So here was Zoe: an intelligent and inquisitive person who suddenly found herself in a place where she saw dead bodies and smelled burning flesh. A place where she experienced both the richness and the destruction of Iraqi culture. And here was Zoe going through all this at a really impressionable age. It would have to result in tremendous personal growth. And in Zoe's case it certainly did.

One day, a HUMINT interrogator approaches me and asks whether I might be willing to assist in interrogations as a female Arabic linguist. I assume he asks because he wishes to interrogate a female prisoner. Or because he simply needs my skills as a linguist. But these assumptions turn out to be wrong.

I'm familiar with the cages. I know about the interrogations. I know we are playing loud rock music day and night to irritate the prisoners. Anything to keep them awake. I know we make prisoners participate in chants of "I love Bush" or "I love America." Anything to piss them off.

When the interrogater and one or two other HUMINT guys coach me on my role for these interrogations, it is not what I expect. Once we get down to the cage area and I cover my nametapes and rank with tape (this is standard practice to prevent retribution), I am told what they will want me to do.

"We are going to bring these guys in. One at a time. Remove their clothes. Strip them naked. Then we will remove the guy's blindfold. And then we want you to say things to humiliate them. Whatever you want. Things to embarrass them. Whatever you can say to humiliate them."

I am surprised by this, but I don't turn around, either. I don't get myself out of there. I want to help—to prevent the kind of thing that has happened to Staff Sergeant Kelly—so I do as I am told.

So I enter the interrogation room. Some HUMINT guys are there along with some other MI guys as guards. There is a civilian interpreter present as well. The sergeant first class in charge of the whole cage is not present.

The prisoner enters the room with a blindfold on and his hands tied behind his back. Things happen like they said they would. They remove his clothes. They position him so he is facing me. When they remove the blindfold, I am the first person he sees.

The civilian interpreter and the interrogator (who also speaks Arabic) mock the prisoner. Mock his manhood. Mock his sexual prowess. Ridicule the size of his genitals. Point to me. Remind him that he is being humiliated in the presence of this blond American female. Anything. Anything that comes to mind.

Degrade the prisoner. Try to break him down. Try to break

his spirit. Occasionally they also ask questions on topics that might have some possible Intel value.

I am watching this, and it is my perception that the Intel value of this prisoner is very limited. However, I am not in a position to judge. I am not in a position to make this assessment. I haven't read the files.

I am prompted to participate. To mock this naked and crying man.

What do I say? What can I say?

"Do you think you can please a woman with that thing?" I ask, gesturing.

I have no aptitude for this work. I prove almost immediately that I am no good at this.

I tell him he had better tell us what we want to know, or we won't stop. But I am almost feeling pity.

What do you say to someone to make them feel like shit? It's just not something I've ever really *practiced* in my personal life. It is not anything I've ever studied how to do. I'm sure there must be plenty of women who would probably know exactly what to say, but I discover that I am actually not one of them.

It is all odd and uncomfortable. But I don't know enough about what it is the HUMINT people do to know whether what I am seeing is what is supposed to happen.

Soldiers flick lit cigarette butts at the prisoner.

It's one thing to make fun of someone and attempt to humiliate him. With words. That's one thing. But flicking lit cigarettes at somebody—like *burning* him—that's illegal.

It's a violation of the Geneva Conventions.

They smack the prisoner across the face.

These actions definitely cross a line.

While I am watching them do these things to this prisoner, I think a lot about Rick. I imagine what it would be like for him in a situation like this. Especially with a woman there to watch. How much it would distress him. The face is not the same, but the prisoner's eyes look a lot like Rick's. The same shape of eyes, the same eye color. The same lashes.

What would it be like for Rick if he ever went home to Palestine and got picked up for any reason by the Israelis and treated this way? What would it be like for him? As I watch, I imagine Rick. I imagine Rick *in this room.*

That becomes about the only thing I think about while everything else is going on. I'm no longer trying to contribute. I'm not insulting the prisoner or trying to mock him. I've fallen silent. But no one notices, because I am still a useful prop. No one seems to mind that I have nothing to say.

When it's over after one more prisoner and a couple of hours, I tell the interrogator that I do not want to do this again.

Then I tell him that what we are doing to the prisoners in these cages is a violation of the Geneva Conventions. (I know this because the Army repeatedly gives us refresher courses on the Geneva Conventions.) I tell him it's illegal to burn prisoners—or smack them.

He does not appear surprised or bothered by what I say.

"Yes," he says. "But you have to know that these people are criminals. This is the only way to deal with them. You know these people only respect strength, power. Under Saddam it was so much worse for them. They'll never listen to us unless we play rough. Besides, the terrorists don't follow the Geneva Conventions—so why should we?"

I say to him: "But you do know that not all these guys are terrorists."

"Sure," he says casually. "Yeah. I know."

"And you know," I add, "that if one of these guys does not walk in here a terrorist, he is going to walk out of here a terrorist."

"Yeah," this NCO says calmly. "Sure. I know that."

After that day I avoid the cages. There's a phone in the office that we can all use for free. To call the States or whatever. I do not go down there to use it often. I don't want to see things that will disturb me. More of the sort of things I've already seen. This building has a courtyard in the middle. When you walk through the area to get to the office phone, you can see into the courtyard. And then you can't help seeing prisoners getting handled roughly—shoved around while blindfolded, forced to do exercises, like the knee bender, for long periods of time.

At a later time the cage where I witnessed these abuses got investigated. A prisoner died in custody there. Another prisoner had a broken jaw. A third prisoner complained to authorities that he had been burned with cigarettes.

So it wasn't only the Abu Ghraib prison near Baghdad where abuses occurred in Iraq at the end of 2003. It was a bigger problem than that.

Later I spoke with one of the officers who had been in charge of a cage in Mosul. He now said that he would conduct interrogations very differently after the revelations of torture at Abu Ghraib. In the fall of 2003, he said, he had definitely been under the impression that just about *any* interrogation procedure was authorized because we were dealing with terrorists. He had been given the firm impression that this had been put out at the highest levels—from George W. Bush and Donald Rumsfeld on down. That the old rules no longer applied because this was a different world. This was a new kind of war.

Later, of course, there would be these huge investigations. All the paperwork would be requested for review. Everything would be gone through again and again. Now the officer told me that if he were ever to return to Iraq, everything would have to be done very differently.

Later, when I was back in the States, I spoke with a HUMINT female who had been present on a routine basis at these interrogations at this compound in Mosul. That had been her job. She had helped to conduct these interrogations almost every day over a period of several months.

This was sometime in late spring of 2004, around the time the Abu Ghraib prisoner-abuse scandal was breaking. I met her at a cookout with mutual friends in Tennessee. Everything was lush and green in Tennessee at that time of year. Verdant. Iraq felt far away.

I mentioned something to her in passing about Abu Ghraib. Her response was simple:

"I don't see the problem with anything that occurred in those interrogations," she told me. "I don't see a problem with anything those soldiers did."

I was horrified when she said this. I have not been able to have a normal conversation with her since. I still don't even know how to *look* at her.

No one should be allowed to do interrogations every day for as long as our interrogators had been required to do them. It fucks you up in ways we can only guess.

Look at the people who volunteered off the streets to participate in a famous university study in which they were told to play the roles of prisoners and guards. These participants in this study *knew* they were part of a study. Yet they immediately moved past the line most of us would consider an acceptable response. These participants revealed a remarkable willingness to inflict pain. They showed a tremendous capacity for hurting and torturing other human beings *for no other reason* than that they had been told to do so. And we're talking about ordinary people who knew that they were participating in a research study.

Now make it for real.

Tell these same ordinary people that if they do a good-enough job as interrogators, if they are able to break prisoners down and get intelligence from them, they might be saving the lives of people they know and friends they work with every day. And then observe how these ordinary people respond.

It has been shown time and again that it is not at all unusual for people to cross a line and do what most of us would consider aberrant.

I guess I interpret my own refusal to continue to participate in those interrogations as, in fact, the more unusual response.

However, I did not file a complaint.

I did not go higher.

I did not do anything to stop those interrogations. I did not stand up and say: "This is not okay. It must stop."

I did not do anything like that. All I said was: "I am not going to be a part of it." I did not blow the whistle on anybody.

So how morally culpable am I?

READING *ATLAS SHRUGGED* IN MOSUL

WHEN YOU HAVE a fight-or-flight response, your adrenaline starts pumping. It takes a tremendous amount of control for your mind not to let your body and its hormones do whatever they want. Which is to respond in a physical way to a threat.

At a certain point we all started to hate the fucking locals. The longer we were there, the more difficult things got.

Zoe and I talked about this.

We had both studied the culture. We spoke the language. We understood at least a little about the religion and the history of the region. We had so much more understanding than the average soldier. And even *we* reached the point where we were very close to hating the Iraqi people.

Infantry guys? And not just infantry, but most Army people there?

A lot of Army people said—and seemed to believe—that we should just nuke the region. Nuke the Middle East. And fuck 'em all. They've been trying to kill each other for a thousand years. Kill 'em all.

Let the whole region be glass.

I heard at least twenty people in the Army say this.

Just nuke it.

Me? Being vaguely nonconfrontational (but not really non-confrontational), I tried a whole range of responses.

I said: "Hey, come on, there's innocent women and children here."

And I got back: "Nobody here is innocent. If they're not little killers now, they're gonna grow up to be killers."

So I said: "But you know we're here for the oil, right? And if you nuke Iraq, it'll all be radioactive. And we won't be able to come and get the oil."

And the response was: "Yeah, whatever. Technology will figure it out. They'll figure out a way to be able to do it. It'll be okay."

Understand that these were *not* bad people. These were simply people who were *beyond* frustrated. Beyond angry. Beyond bitter.

Soldiers were put in these impossible situations. For a while, 3rd Brigade's job was propane distribution. They manned points where they passed out propane. These were *soldiers*. Their mission was to fight and win our nation's wars. That is the Army's mission statement. And here were soldiers passing out free tanks of propane to people so they could cook or whatever.

So these soldiers were doing a good thing for people, and then they watched while locals cut in line and shoved little kids out of the way. And sometimes the soldiers reached a breaking point where they just grabbed somebody's empty tank—and chucked it. Just threw it. *If you can't play by the rules, fuck you.*

Whenever I saw prisoners who had been roughed up before they were put in the cage, I never criticized the infantry because they were in extraordinarily stressful situations. These guys were getting shot at all the time. They might have watched their friends die. They're out there in the shit every day. So definitely they responded with more violence. When they arrested some-body, they knocked them around a little. Dealt with them harshly. And I didn't feel like I was in a place to criticize. But if once the prisoners' hands were tied and they were in a secure location, and MI people—or MPs—engaged in that kind of behavior, I did not feel they had any excuse.

You have a higher moral responsibility to treat somebody appropriately when you're a prison guard than when you're an arresting officer. When you are not worried that they might try to kill you. When you are not worried that their family could pour out of a building and shoot you.

Matt told me about these times he was manning Traffic Control Points (TCP). And he injured people. Hit people. Busted out car windows of locals who were behaving inappropri-ately. And part of it was that he could. He had the power to do it. But part of it was *he was scared.*

And people overreact when they're scared.

It took Matt more than a year before he told me this story about manning a TCP.

"Things would get kind of messy sometimes. We'd string c-wire across the point, and we'd check cars and stuff. There was this one dude who decided to get lippy with this one officer at one point. So the officer made him empty out the entire back of his truck. The dude had all these crates of fruit. And the officer made him empty every piece of fruit off his truck. And so he's pulling off the very last piece, and the officer was like: 'Okay, you can put it all back.' It took this Iraqi four hours to unload and load his truck. Making real sure he wouldn't get an attitude the next time he got to a TCP.

"We were doing twenty-four-hour TCPs when there were reports that Saddam was in the area. Basically we stopped the Iraqis and searched their cars. Then sent them on their way. A few times a car heading toward us would start to turn around. They'd see us and then go back, turning away from the checkpoint. And we opened up with our weapons. Assuming they had something to hide. And might be a threat. Did I ever hit anybody? I don't know. One car, we *had* to have killed some locals. I can't imagine we didn't—we opened up with machine guns. The entire platoon opened up on this one truck. Actually it was pretty funny. There was nothing left of the truck. Another time this other guy I knew killed a local guy and a little kid. Another dude in that car actually lived. I have no idea how he lived, because there were bullet holes everywhere. Good times."

Sometime earlier that fall I spent a month at Range 54 at the base of the mountains outside Sinjar. It was not as secure as the Tal Afar airfield base, but it was relatively secure. There were gates and guards, but it wasn't as built-up as the airfield base. And it was smaller. Range 54 was 2/187's site.

Matt was there as part of a fire support team. By that point I trusted Matt deeply. It was at Range 54 that Matt gave me a metal police baton he had acquired, calling it his "*hajji*-be-good stick."

At Range 54 we worked indoors in a building. And we slept indoors for the first time in many months. There was no hot running water. A shower was a rigged thing that resembled an outhouse. And we also had an outhouse for a toilet. But the outhouse was an improvement because it wasn't a hole in the ground. It did, however, bug me that the guys left their porn regularly in the outhouses—left open to the appropriate page beside a tube of lotion.

One of the FISTers actually confessed to me at some point that it was difficult for him to shit in an outhouse after several months of squatting. He told me: "When I first got back in to the airfield? I'd climb up on the platform of the seat in these outhouses and I'd squat on 'em. 'Cause I couldn't otherwise." Now you have to understand two things about this story: (1) What he said made complete sense to me, and (2) this was a perfectly acceptable topic of conversation by this point in our deployment.

At Range 54 the locals burned our shit for us. Stirred it up with diesel fuel and lit it. For four dollars a day. I assisted with translation to give the locals instructions on what work needed to get done.

That's why Matt gave me the *hajji*-be-good stick. Some of the locals (who drove the buses) slept right behind the building where I slept. Matt didn't trust them. So he wanted to be sure I'd be safe. That's why he gave me the stick to keep under my pillow at night.

At that location I was one of four females out of five hundred people. This was intimidating. And I dealt with it by not making friends with guys there. I became less outgoing, less friendly, less revealing of personal information.

I was already friends with Matt, and I let the other guys assume that because he and I were friends that he *owned* me. I did nothing to correct this assumption. You didn't mess with another guy's girl.

So I got left alone more. I got time to think.

I thought about the mountain time when I was alone mainly with guys I knew and liked. And I thought about the incident with Rivers. It sharpened my focus.

For the longest time I continued to feel so responsible, wondering whether I had encouraged Rivers by being friendly and outgoing. By my willingness to talk about sex with him. By talking about relationships and personal things with guys I didn't know so well. Did I set myself up?

Was it my fault? Was I asking for it?

So I decided to change my behavior. I wasn't so friendly anymore. I kept myself to myself.

I was also coming into a fuller sense of my own abilities and strengths. I was really coming to believe in myself. My confidence, my sense of what I could do, had developed so much that when I was made a team leader—in September 2003—I was really happy. I was thrilled. I felt ready and comfortable moving into a leadership position.

Admittedly my team was me and only one other soldier. By this point in our deployment, there were very few people in my platoon. Our ranks had been seriously reduced due to ETS and PCS. When we left Fort Campbell in January, we had two Prophet teams of four people each in my platoon, a low-level voice intercept (LLVI) team of four people, and a Prophet Control team with six people that did analysis of our data. By this point, there was one two-person Prophet team, one four-man LLVI team, and one three-person Prophet Control team. And that was it.

It was difficult. For one thing we should still have been pulling twenty-four-hour ops. But a team of two soldiers couldn't manage that. We shut down midnight to six.

I was still motivated to get my soldier into shape. He arrived overweight, so I developed a PT program for him. Clearly he had not been responsible for himself, and I went out of my way to find other training opportunities for him.

Since my promotion had not gone through yet, the soldier on my team and I were the same rank. A male friend of mine whose team leader was a girl and also the same rank had already told me that when people came to his site, they would talk to him—not to his team leader. And that would bother him.

He would say: "She's the team leader."

People would say: "Uh-huh. Yeah. Okay." And then keep talking to him. And repeatedly address him as if he were in charge.

He would again say: "No, no. *She's* in charge."

Now the same thing happened to me.

When people came up to our site, they addressed the soldier on my team.

And I had to say, "Excuse me. You know *I'm* in charge. *I'm* the team leader."

Possibly due to my months of solitude, and possibly due to the Rivers incident, I started to pay attention to how females were getting treated. Now there were MKTs (mobile kitchen trailers) at Range 54, so instead of always having MREs, we filed through a line into a shelter and got hot food. Everyone stared at the few women.

And then there was the time I decided to wear mascara to a Bruce Willis concert at Tal Afar. I didn't think about it beforehand. It was a concert. So I put on the mascara, and I honestly did not think anyone would notice.

Everyone noticed.

This guy I knew who *wasn't* at the concert saw me a few weeks later.

"Hey, Kayla, I heard you wore mascara to the Bruce Willis concert."

I could not believe it.

I saw a number of soldiers in my company again, soldiers I had not seen very much since we all left Fort Campbell. And my team was spending a lot more time at the airfield by this time, so there was more time to hang out with the guys in my company. I also saw other MI females in my unit, and we caught up on things. I started hearing gossip from infantry guys about girls. I had no idea how much (if any) of the gossip was true. But I started to hear all kinds of stuff.

"Oh, you're on a Prophet team? Hey, we heard from this guy that we know about this girl on another Prophet Team who sucked his cock in the back of a Humvee."

"You're an MI girl on a Prophet team? Okay. We know about girls like you."

"You know Janice? She's on this other Prophet team? I heard she let a group of guys run a train on her. You know what I mean, right? She pretty much spread her legs while they lined up and took turns. All you girls do that?"

Dammit.

No doubt guys were getting antsy. Bored. By that point the main combat effort was over. Combat really focused our attention. Now we were more settled into locations where we had less movement and fewer missions. So guys started to think a little more about what they weren't getting. At that point we had a little more access to phones. We could occasionally get on the

Internet and check our e-mail. So guys were thinking about home more often. Stuff like that.

So it was around this time that I really began to think about how I was presenting myself to other people.

It was also around this time that I first heard that a female in the Army deployed in Iraq was either a bitch or a slut. That that was the choice we faced.

That was when I began to think: I would rather be a bitch.

And then Staff Sergeant Simmons arrived. When she wasn't busy flirting with infantry guys, she'd take down her long black hair and brush it. And brush it. And brush it. Or whenever a guy walked into our area, she would also take down her hair and brush it. She smoked these long and skinny freakish-smelling cig- arettes. Then she'd ash them into half-full water bottles she never capped. After a short while, there were these half-full water bottles with cigarette butts and ashes everywhere.

SSG Simmons outranked me and took over my team. Meeting her, and disliking her, I thought a lot more about how even one horrible female soldier affected how the men saw *all* female soldiers.

Probably some of my initial response to her was territorial. Territorial about my team, my stuff, my job. I probably didn't want to give up my newfound sense of authority and responsibil- ity. After all, I'd signed for all the equipment, and now SSG Simmons came along and wanted to touch things.

When she arrived, I was signed for 1.3 million dollars' worth of equipment. I was signed for our truck. I was signed for three laptops. I was signed for all our equipment. This amounted to nearly two hundred discrete items. Everything had a line item, and it was not easy to keep everything straight. Since this was the fucking Army, every item had its own number and letter. MA711-Charlie? This? I had to learn what every letter and number meant.

When I signed for it from the sergeant before me, he didn't know what everything was. When he signed for it from the sergeant before him, she didn't know what everything was, either. But I had been told that you were not supposed to sign for anything unless you absolutely knew that everything was there. But on the day I started to figure everything out, it got dark, so I said, "Fuck it," and signed for the rest. Then I spent two days laying every single piece of equipment out all over the floor and figuring out what every single item was. Then I put everything related to the solar charging panel into one Baggie, and everything related to something else into another Baggie.

It was a huge pain in the ass.

Now here's SSG Simmons rustling around in my fucking shit. Moving stuff around. No clue what anything is, but feeling free to mess with my organization because she can. Because she's technically in charge now.

She almost immediately pisses everyone off when she decides on her 4:00 A.M. shift to sweep the small building where we live, work, and sleep. We are all still sleeping, and choking clouds of dust wake us up.

For no apparent reason Simmons has laid out a box of books that had been neatly stacked inside a crate. So now all the books are dusty. But that's the least of it.

Our technician says to her: "Please. We have extremely sensitive equipment in here. Do not sweep unless you bag the laptop.

You have to put it inside a plastic bag. To keep the dust from damaging it."

She never does this. She never listens.

"Isn't it great how I did this? Isn't it great how I reorganized everything? It looks so much prettier."

Once Staff Sergeant Simmons announces to Matt that he should bring his infantry friends over to play cards.

She tells him: "Don't worry. I won't bite . . . unless you want me to." (Matt turns her down politely enough to her face, but he tells me later he can't stand that "scary troll bitch.")

SSG Simmons announces to everyone that she's planning to cheat on Simmons, her second husband.

She also never bothers to learn anything about Iraq.

When she first shows up, she asks me: "Can you tell me where we are in the world? What are the neighboring countries? What are the ethnic groups here? What are the religious groups here? Why are we in Iraq? Tell me why we are here."

Not knowing how to respond, I make an attempt at humor: "Oh, ha-ha-ha. No one knows why we're here! You know those weapons of mass destruction—"

"Weapons? Of mass destruction?"

And I think: Oh, my God. She really doesn't know.

So here is this woman in charge of my team in a country where she has been sent to fight and possibly even to die. And she has not bothered to pick up a newspaper or do any basic research. She has no idea what she's doing here.

Staff Sergeant Simmons's cluelessness and lack of motivation crush me.

I am feeling: Enough already with the bad female leadership.

I am starting to feel cursed by God.

———

I leave SSG Simmons and my unit in late October to have my foot surgery in Mosul. Once I've recovered I stay in Tal Afar at the airfield because my team has already left Range 54 on a new mission to work with new equipment. I request to stay at the airfield until I'm off my crutches. Then I rejoin my team at 2nd Brigade's BSA in Mosul, where I stay for the remainder of my deployment.

My time away from SSG Simmons makes nothing better.

In Mosul we get mortared on a regular basis. It is crucial always to tell someone where you are going, how long you plan to be gone, when you plan to return, and so on. That's just common sense. You don't scamper off on your own in a damned combat zone and go do whatever the fuck you please. You tell somebody: "I'm going to chow. I'll be back within an hour."

SSG Simmons does not do this. She makes friends, and she disappears to have visits to watch movies, or whatever. Gone for any number of hours. Without telling any of us where she's going. Or when she's coming back.

A couple of times we're mortared, and the command higher up insists on 100 percent accountability checks. When you verify that everybody in your unit is still alive. And she's just nowhere to be found. If a lower enlisted private did something like that, that person would be in a lot of trouble. But she just slides by.

Things keep getting worse and worse. Staff Sergeant Simmons refuses to learn the equipment. I constantly have to struggle to make sure that the mission is happening. It is an effort all the time. I have to do a lot of things that are supposed to be her responsibility. So I begin to communicate directly with her superior to get the information I need to do my job.

When she learns this, her position is clear.

"You must stop usurping my authority. You are not allowed to have any communication with anybody that does not go directly through me."

It becomes a big problem. SSG Simmons makes it clear that she plans to recommend me for disciplinary action. For insubordination.

My platoon sergeant is very vocal if he believes you are bad at something.

He will tell you: "You're fucked up. You're a shitbag. You are not doing what you are supposed to do. Why don't you know this? What the fuck is the matter with you?"

But he is never vocal about praise.

He will not say to you: "Hey, you're a good soldier. You really know your shit. You're really squared away and you're a good leader."

He does not volunteer positive reinforcement. It's not what he does.

So there's only one way I ever know that he thinks well of me.

When you're a low-ranking enlisted soldier—E-4 or below—you are supposed to get a monthly counseling statement. It tells you what you're doing and what you're supposed to be doing. It's a professional development sort of thing to help you be a better soldier.

Once you become a noncommissioned officer, you get an NCOER—that is, a noncommissioned officer evaluation report. These have to be done yearly or every time you have a change of rater. So every time you get a new boss, your old boss is obligated to do one of these on you. If you get a negative NCOER, it will seriously impact your chances for getting promoted again.

So since Staff Sergeant Simmons is in charge of me, she should be writing an NCOER on me whenever I finally leave her team for my own.

I am quite concerned. So I speak to my platoon sergeant.

"What am I going to do? She's going to give me a bad NCOER—and it's going to mess up my entire Army career."

"No," he tells me. "Don't worry. She will *never* do an NCOER on you. I have made clear to her that you are a team leader and she is a team leader. And that therefore I will rate you. I'm your rater. Not her."

It's a really big deal. He is not going to let her get away with this.

That's the only way I ever know that my platoon sergeant thinks I'm worth a shit.

Finally, sometime around Christmas, things get so bad that SSG Simmons and I end up sitting down together with a lieutenant to mediate our discussion. I want a witness so she cannot claim that I am out of line.

I begin.

"Look, I am not sure that you understand what is going on. And I want to make sure that you are clear on the fact that I am *not* trying to hurt you or your career. I am not trying to usurp your authority. I am trying to help you because you are in charge. If shit is fucked up, it is not me who looks bad. It is you who looks bad. If the mission does not get accomplished, you look bad because you're in charge. Me making sure the mission happens is not me trying to make you look bad. It's me trying to save your ass. It's me trying to make sure that the things you are supposed to accomplish are accomplished *on time* and *to standard*. That's me trying to help you—not me trying to hurt you. I'm trying to talk to you about these things because I feel communication has gotten very poor. And I have to do something because that's not okay. It's not working."

She says: "I really appreciate you coming forward. And making the effort. Taking the initiative. And while we're talking about things, I want to tell you that I feel you don't respect me because you know I don't care about learning anything about the technical side of our job. Or learning anything about our equipment."

This blows my mind.

Well, I want to say. *Yeah.*

But I can't say this, of course. So I just kind of stare at her.

And the lieutenant is staring at her by this point as well. Jaw slightly agape.

Is she honestly saying this to us? As a *defense* for her not knowing her job?

Then she says it again.

"I really am feeling you don't respect me because I don't care about learning about the technical aspects of our job."

And I am looking at her. Searching for words.

"It's important for you to be able to identify the equipment that you are signed for."

She has signed for more than a million dollars' worth of equipment. If it gets lost or broken through an act of negligence—like dropping it in a river or smashing it with a bat or whatever—she is responsible for it. And the Army can take money out of her paycheck.

"Oh," she says, huffily. "So I guess this is going to be the time to just rip on me. And bring up all my faults."

"I . . . " I begin. ". . . don't, um, know . . . how to have this conversation anymore."

———

A month or so later we drive to Kuwait, where we will live in these fifteen-hundred-person warehouses with bunk cots. Just waiting to go back to the States.

There's been this general announcement: *Maintain positive control of your sensitive items.* Like your weapon. You do not lose your fucking weapon. And your night vision goggles are another sensitive item. You must be accountable for them at all times. But people are told to throw their rucksacks onto large baggage trucks to be transported to the warehouses.

When no one is looking, SSG Simmons chucks her NVGs up into the baggage truck with everyone's bags.

Later the people who unpack the trucks find them.

"So whose are these?"

When the commander learns that the NVGs belong to SSG Simmons, she gets severely chastised.

"What are you thinking? What are you doing? What the fuck is wrong with you?"

Simmons sits on her cot and cries. In front of everyone.

And in front of everyone, she blames her crying on PMS. Yet another thing that is absolutely not acceptable in the Army. It encourages men to think what most men think already: that PMS makes girls do incompetent things. Which I prefer to think is not true. Because you still hear lots of stuff like, *Women should never be president because they're too emotional to handle it. What if she got PMS, she'd start a nuclear war!*

People remain concerned about women in leadership roles. So for SSG Simmons to have her breakdown in public does *not* help.

I am horrified. Zoe and I are both horrified.

This woman's incompetence makes all women in the Army look incompetent.

We had a lot of downtime in Iraq. There was plenty of time to read. I probably read two hundred books during my year of deployment.

I started reading Ayn Rand's *Atlas Shrugged* at Range 54. It took me forever to read. I didn't actually finish it until I was at 2nd Brigade in Mosul. Reading *Atlas Shrugged* in Mosul ended up being a very formative experience.

Rand is all about personal responsibility. In a lot of ways she's an intellectual snob. A tremendous elitist. There's a sentiment expressed by a central character in *Atlas Shrugged*. She talks about how she has to struggle *against* other people to get her job done. It's hard enough to do her job, but then she also has to actively fight people who appear to be trying to prevent work from happening. She talks about how frustrating it can be to deal with incompetence. How exhausting and draining it can be.

I identified strongly with this.

Rand's books are also rants against communism. They document all the things that are wrong with communism and how it can ruin people's lives.

And I identified with this as well.

Reading *Atlas Shrugged* in Mosul, I became convinced that the Army was really this vast communist institution in disguise. I don't mean "communist" in the sense of sharing what you have, getting what you need. I don't mean "communist" in the sense of equality for all. Not that utopian bullshit.

I mean real-world communism. The fucked-up kind.

In real-world communism, folks did as little as possible to get as much as possible. They scammed their way up the bureaucratic ladder. They said to themselves: "There is the hard way, the right way, and the way to get whatever I fucking want without doing anything at all." Door number three, please.

Because so often in the Army, your pay was not related to how hard you worked. That's what I figured out from reading Rand. Because someone else around you was not doing anything—and they were still getting the same amount of money as you. Or more. And if you did work harder, you just ended up feeling like you were getting screwed. In this way the Army encouraged people to do as little as possible. Of course, not everyone was this way—but it was depressingly common.

This was a powerful revelation because I was realizing how good I was at my job and how hard I worked. And here I was again faced with someone in charge of me who was not good at her job and did not work hard. Here I was stuck with yet another completely incompetent team leader. Feeling this severe frustration.

I began to feel wistfully like it should be permitted to dispose of my team leader. Get her out of my way.

I returned to the Tal Afar airfield for Christmas. To be around people I liked and to get away from Staff Sergeant Simmons. By this point there were trailers at the airfield, and almost everyone was living indoors with heat, which was really nice. It had already started to get cold in November.

By this point they had all these chow halls, courtesy of Halliburton. (By now Halliburton had the contract for building all the chow halls over there. They ended up getting investigated for not meeting their contract—for not providing a certain number of meals to a certain number of soldiers a certain number of times a day. Meanwhile they imported foreign workers to serve us food in these nice shiny buildings. So there were these Pakistani workers at Tal Afar and all these cute little Filipina girls working in Mosul. It was pretty peculiar.)

On Christmas we got a really nice meal. But on the way to the chow hall in the parking lot there were civil affairs and psyop vehicles with mounted speakers. Usually these vehicles would drive through the towns broadcasting warnings or information. Now the Army vehicles were blasting Christmas carols. It was an unreal sight.

On Christmas they showed us a DVD. Shots of people's loved ones back at Fort Campbell holding up signs like HONK, IF YOU SUPPORT OUR TROOPS. And you saw all the cars driving by and honking. You saw children holding up signs like I LOVE MY DADDY. Kids holding up signs that said what unit their dad was in. Everyone waving American flags.

An overweight interpreter named Rob put on a Santa suit. Our first sergeant, our commander, my platoon sergeant, and this guy, Rob, went around and gave everyone a stocking with random Christmasy things like soap and candy.

The videotape and the stockings were surprisingly emotional for me. I started thinking about my own family. About them worrying about me. And missing me.

All this footage of people at home lining the roads and cheering us.

I started to cry, alone in my trailer.

SITUATION NORMAL

When my tour was coming to an end, I got my truck back and had two soldiers under me while we drove all the way from Mosul to Kuwait. We had major mechanical problems with our truck; we had no lights, and our radios were down. At night, I clipped a little flashlight to my sleeve, and when I had to brake, I'd stick my little light out the window so the truck behind me could see me. That was my brake light. The only communication we had was a handheld Motorola with which we could speak with the truck in front of us (that also had a handheld Motorola). The only radios we had were radios we'd purchased with our own money. The entire drive was basically horrible, but once it was over it was great.

At the end there came the moment when we finally saw the berm that separated Iraq from Kuwait. As my first sergeant would say, seeing the berm was a significant emotional event. He liked to say: "There are going to be a lot of significant emotional events for people here." (I also thought of that phrase the day I washed out Lott's bloody gear. The day Berenger died. And I thought of it again then.) It was exactly that—a significant emotional event. We crossed the berm. We survived. We made it out of Iraq alive.

A couple of miles past the berm, we stopped to refuel. And we took off our flak vests. From that point on, we could drive around without those hot fucking things on. That too was a significant emotional event.

Guys were lighting cigars. A lot of people were taking pictures. People were hugging.

We spent the next two or three weeks in Kuwait at an established U.S. Army base. Time to decompress that was very important. We cleaned our trucks and cleaned our equipment. Got everything packed and ready to go on the ships. But we also got to go shopping for souvenirs and wander around and get doughnuts, Chinese food, pizza. Drink near-beer. Use the phone. Check our e-mail. We were able to do pseudo-American things for a little while.

During this time in Kuwait, we were also not allowed to carry around a weapon. I spent nearly the entire time in Kuwait reaching for my carbine no matter where I was. I'd get up from the chow hall in a frantic panic, afraid I'd lost it.

I came home on February 8, 2004. It was snowing lightly at Fort Campbell. It had been almost exactly one year since I'd been here, and it had been snowing when I left. Small sharp flakes that stung the face. I had a surreal moment of feeling like I'd never left; that it had all been a sick dream—or as if, somehow, I had just lost a whole year of my life. There had been this gap in the normal passage of time, and then it fitfully resumed right where it had left off.

The night I got home, I got in touch with Shane Kelly. He had returned to Fort Campbell in January after three months at Walter Reed Army Medical Center. And after that first night, we hung out together all the time.

I was incredibly happy to be back in America. But for the longest time, I did not want to be around non-Army people. And I kept having feelings of wanting to be back there.

When you come home, you spend a lot of time talking about how you want to get back to Iraq. You feel this guilt for not being with your brothers. For not being with *your people*. The people in your unit. You feel like you're still supposed to be there.

You're not done.

I remembered that when I spoke to anybody who took mid-tour leave, they had expressed similar feelings. And now I felt them, too.

There was culture shock.

Everyone in America was fat. Everyone was on some stupid diet. How could a diet encourage you to eat bacon and forbid you to eat bananas? It made no sense to me. I felt like people didn't understand anything. That they were selfish and didn't appreciate what they had.

I came home, and the only things people were interested in were things just beyond my comprehension. Who cared about Jennifer Lopez? How was it that I was watching CNN one morning and there was a story about freaking ducklings being fished out of a damn sewer drain—while the story of soldiers getting killed in Iraq got relegated to this little banner across the bottom of the screen? Ducklings getting pulled out of a sewer. How was this important to our country?

I was not understanding what was going on. I was not grasping anything.

How was I willing to go and die for these fucking people who wear sweatshirts with little kittens on them? Or these people with sequins who bump into me with their carts at the supermarket and then look at me like I'm an asshole?

It's a very strange country we live in.

I felt thoroughly out of place. I felt this jarring sense of *I do not belong here.*

Soon after my return I visited my father and stepmother in North Carolina.

The big talk on their block was the glorified mobile home that was being put in their gated community. The neighbors were up in arms over this. Oh my God! The world is coming to an end! This prefab home does not meet the ideal standards of life in the community!

Everyone was aghast. "What about property values?"

I thought: Who are you people? You people are all *rich.* You have electricity. You have phones. I just came back from a place where people wanted my cardboard boxes for flooring. What the fuck is wrong with you?

My parents were supportive. They were fine.

But everywhere we went, it was always the same.

"This is my daughter. She just got back from Iraq."

"Oh, thank you! Thank you!" And then it was always the same question. "What was it like?"

I understood people were saying this to be nice. But what could I say? What was I supposed to say?

"Well, while I was in Mosul, this sergeant major and his driver got pulled out of their vehicle by a mob and their bodies were literally torn apart. So how's your year been?"

What am I supposed to say?

"Oh, yeah. I watched a guy bleed to death. And I smelled burning shit all the time. It was super."

I didn't know how to deal with people.

My parents' mailman sent me magazines while I was in Iraq. My parents told him that magazines were what I wanted most. So he took it upon himself as his project to collect magazines from all the people on his route. He boxed them up and shipped them to me at his own expense. Sometimes when my parents shipped me things, he just paid for it.

I sent him a thank-you note.

When I got to North Carolina, he stopped by for a visit.

It turned out he was a Vietnam vet.

So I thanked him all over again for the magazines and everything. He told me the letter I sent to him from Iraq thanking him meant more to him than a letter from the president would have meant to him. My letter was just that important and moving to him.

And he told me: "You know, the welcome home that you troops coming back from Iraq are getting is like the recognition we never got. I feel like it's for me too. For me and all Vietnam vets."

He went on about my sacrifice and how important it was that I went to war.

I didn't know how to react to him at all.

Here's a guy who also told me that all but two soldiers in his platoon got killed in Vietnam.

Not one person in my entire company was killed in Iraq. At the time I returned only four hundred American military had died in Iraq. Four hundred soldiers died every week in Vietnam.

I didn't feel like I deserved any of what he told me. At all. I felt like it was wrong. I did not go through anything like what he had gone through.

So for me to think that what I experienced in Iraq was tough or difficult—compared with what this guy went through in Vietnam—felt wrong. Nothing I experienced was as bad as that.

I felt guilty that he treated me so well.

Guilty that he acted like I was so great or did such a great thing.

Like I didn't deserve his praise. It was just awkward.

So you get home and you are supposed to want to be home and you are supposed to be so happy to see your family—and then all you want is to get back to Army people.

I could only handle being home for three or four days.

I ended up fleeing so I didn't have to deal with my own family or civilians. So I went back to Fort Campbell. Where it was easier. Where everyone understood. Where no one asked questions. Where it was easier to talk with other people because they'd been there too. Where you didn't have to explain a lot of things. Back to *people who knew*. It was so much simpler.

I couldn't cope with the rest of it. I didn't want to cope with the rest of it.

At some point I accompanied Shane when he visited his family, and that was also super-awkward. All the attention when his mom told everyone: "This is my son. And he just got back from Iraq."

Even a year after he returned, she still put it the same way.

"This is my son. He just got back from Iraq."

My parents did the same thing for almost a year after I returned.

"No," I'd say. "I did not just get back anymore. It's been awhile."

No more apologies. That's what being in the Army has taught me when all is said and done. I used to be this girl, like so many girls— I mean studies have been done on this, if you don't want to take my word for it—we *qualify* everything we say. This was me: "I kinda think maybe I'd like sorta to do X or Y. I'm not sure. You decide." With a guy I was the same way. Maybe he'd just fucking *lied* to me. And maybe I'd just caught him at it. But it was still me saying: "I'm sorry." Girls do this all the time. I did it all the time.

I also remember clearly that before I went to Iraq, I always made statements that sounded like questions. When I first arrived at Fort Campbell, for instance, I went into my platoon's office and said: "Um, I think we have formation?" (Though of course I *knew* we had formation). And people didn't get up and go to formation. They went and checked. I spoke like that all the time, and it pissed me off at myself. I should have been more assertive. I also should have been less embarrassed about being smart. Less ashamed of my ability to do things well.

When women are good at what they do, they are not characterized as assertive. They are accused of being ballbusters or bitches. This is a struggle that is magnified in the military because it is still such a male environment—a weird little microcosm of society on steroids.

In a combat zone I couldn't be hesitant. I had to be assured. I couldn't just quit. If you decide to quit in a combat zone, you will probably die. I had to keep going. *I had to do it.* And all of a sudden I realized that the mind is incredibly powerful. I *could* do it. I could do almost anything. I could keep going in situations that I certainly imagined before would have broken me. In Iraq I figured out there was no option for me to do anything else but push myself. And keep pushing.

Which I did. Which I've done.

I felt a lot of clarity while I was in Iraq in terms of my personal life. I really felt a sense of what I wanted out of life. And who I was and where I was going. Maybe this was because my lane was so narrow.

Another Army expression: "Stay in your lane." They say it on the firing range. "Watch your lane. Watch your lane only." So you only fire at the targets in your lane. You stay in your lane. And I always thought this was a great Army phrase. (Civilians should use it at work when somebody gets in their business and they have no reason to do so.) Don't try to get involved in things that don't concern you and that you don't know anything about. For instance, I hate it when somebody corrects my soldiers when I am present. If their uniforms are messed up, that's my business. I have either noticed it and plan to deal with it, or I know a reason for it. Whatever it is, it's my business. Nobody else's business. They need to stay in their lane. In general, I think this is good advice in life.

So in Iraq my lane was very narrow. It became very easy to feel like I knew what I was doing and what was going on. Staying alive. Doing my mission. That was my lane.

Now that I was back in the States, everything opened up. I had to check my private e-mail and my work e-mail. I had to know my password for my e-mail and memorize my PIN number for my bank account and my password for my retirement account. My lane was suddenly huge. I had to deal with friends and family and all sorts of personal questions. I had to pick out what color socks I wanted to wear. And I began to feel like a lot of the clarity I felt and the sense of purpose I had in Iraq had really faded.

While I was in Iraq, everything was clear. I wanted to become a journalist. I wanted to go to graduate school and get a master's degree. I wanted to become a Middle East correspondent for National Public Radio. That was what I wanted to do with my life. So I'd apply to Georgetown University—the worst thing they could do was turn me down. There were no fucking explosives if it didn't work out.

Back home, all that clarity of purpose faded almost before I knew it. I wanted it back. I wanted that feeling of solidity and strength again.

Not everything was awful.

The summer I returned I attended this huge outdoor rock festival. We're talking about 150,000 hippies in one place at one time. Hippie central. I assumed if I mentioned what I did for a living people would react very negatively. But I was really intrigued when everybody was supportive. People were like, *Wow, thanks.* Or, *Hey, you guys are doing a great job.* Or like, *That's really cool.* Two people—two hippies—actually asked me about joining the military. Asked me if I would recommend it to them. It blew my fucking mind: It was a different world out there than it used to be even ten years ago. When I used to go to Lollapalooza in the nineties there would not have been that kind of support. I might have said I was a soldier and the response would have been very different. *Why are you selling your soul to the government, blah, blah, blah?* It would never have been, *Hey, wow. You're awesome.*

And certainly here in the communities around Campbell, there were signs up everywhere. WELCOME BACK 101ST! WE SUPPORT OUR TROOPS! It was huge. And it was great. People around Campbell backed the troops in a big, big way. Even if they didn't support the war, they supported the troops.

But there have still been these feelings of depression.

Months after I returned, it still felt weird that I didn't have a weapon with me at all times. There were times when I almost felt like I should go buy a handgun because I didn't have a weapon in my house. What if something happened?

Little things like that felt completely normal to me. Like my reaction to bad drivers. If someone cut me off in traffic here in Tennessee, there was this automatic adrenaline surge. I can't imagine how I might have responded if I had been allowed to carry my M-4 carbine with me off the base. I don't mean to make a joke about it, but I almost think there might be one or two fewer bad drivers out there.

I still swerved to avoid trash in the road. In Iraq it could be an IED. A soda can on the side of the road could be an IED. A grocery bag could be an IED.

I had real trouble sleeping. I rarely had trouble before combat. Now I woke up with my sheets soaking wet. And I never remembered my dreams. I didn't remember my dreams for an entire year after I got back.

My first Fourth of July home was horrible. I freaked every time a firecracker went off in my neighborhood. If I watched the fireworks go up, it didn't bother me too much. But if I was looking away and talking to someone when one went up, I jumped every time.

It's been frustrating. I just want these feelings to go away. I just want to be normal.

Now the feelings come and go. Almost by day or week. Sometimes I feel better, sometimes worse. It remains hard for me to meet new people.

Sometimes now I end up around a bunch of soldiers who were also in Iraq, and we can talk about what it was like. We can bond pretty easily. But when I meet random civilians, I feel like they don't understand things.

Sometimes I feel I have failed horribly. Even here. Even now. With this book. I have somehow failed to express what life in war was like for us.

There are so many things that are still really tough for me to discuss. And I keep trying to put my finger on *why*. Even though we, the troops today, are supported like the Vietnam vets were not—we now know it took lies to get us deployed. (WMDs? What WMDs?) And all the problems that are still going on. People trying to kill us all the fucking time. The conflict that continues of how to deal with being there with a spoon in one hand and a gun in the other. Falluja's a complete disaster. The mess hall in Mosul where Zoe and I ate chow twice a day has now been bombed—more than twenty soldiers were killed and dozens more were injured. Tal Afar has blown up. Since the 101st left, it's been a total mess.

The more we know about what brought about this war in the first place, the harder and harder it gets. It was a year of my life. And what the fuck for? What was it all about? Not having an answer for that makes it hard. Makes it feel dirty. It was hard enough to go. I had enough doubts when I went. I knew even then that at least some of it was bullshit.

It makes it really hard to know that I was over there and lived in privation and filth, risking my life. Away from my family and my home. Seeing death. What Shane went through. The fact that the war was based on lies destroys some of the sense of purpose for me. It degrades some of the goodness of our efforts. Not all of the goodness. Especially when I think about the children I saw, attending schools again in places where they had not been able to do so for more than a generation. They were so happy to go to school. Or when kids saw us and they'd cheer for us. That means there's hope. A future. But otherwise, talking about the war and our reasons for going to war remain difficult for me. For us. For every single one of us.

EPILOGUE

I PARTICIPATE IN a field-training exercise with the Rakkasans on the Back-40, a huge swath of forest far from Fort Campbell's built-up installations and barracks. Several thousand soldiers out in the field for several days. Living and sleeping outdoors. Once again I'm with 1/187, and only a handful of us are female. I don't see another woman for days.

On the Back-40 at Fort Campbell, it is miserably cold and rainy. A few dozen soldiers play the "enemy," or OPFOR (opposing force). As we clear buildings in an "Iraqi village," the OPFOR opens fire. Caught in a firefight, I shoot my weapon. All our guns are rigged with blank adapters that sound real—but nothing comes out of the barrels. (Paintball rounds would have been better, but they jam too easily. And they also can bruise you if you get shot in the face at close range.)

I hang with infantry guys I haven't seen since the real war. I see Delta Co soldiers from that day in Baghdad when the Iraqi man died. They still remember me after so much time, and that means a lot to me. And here I am again. Interpreting as commanders or platoon leaders talk to "locals"—who are played by Iraqi Americans hired for the occasion. The situation may sound totally absurdist to outsiders, but I am happier and more relaxed doing this than I have been in months.

I worry at first about war flashbacks. Horror memories. And a few guys do freak. Overreact to the situation. Rough up the Iraqi Americans. Kneel hard on their heads.

I'm fine. My mind is clear. I feel purposeful again, very competent. It catches me by surprise what a total rush it is. But when it's over, my body also aches. My knees are fucking sore. Thinking: I am getting too old for this shit.

In 2005 I know only a few people who plan to reenlist. And only a handful who plan to make careers out of the Army. Most who are choosing to reenlist will do so once—and then get out. It's no secret: The Army is currently experiencing serious retention problems due to the high operations tempo. We all know that everyone who deploys can expect to deploy again. And most of us don't like it.

Zoe's out of the Army now. She had applied for an early school drop, but the Army lost her paperwork. She was convinced the drop would never go through. Then—suddenly—it did. And she learned that her contract with the Army would end in less than two weeks. Of course she was relieved. But also scared. How was she going to support herself? Getting out so fast meant she would not get monthly paychecks she'd been expecting. And now she had to deal with that. Not to mention everything else. No more life insurance. No more health insurance. No more access to the commissary. She wouldn't be able to go to the cheap mechanics on base if her car broke down. Zoe's now attending college full-time with an idea that she might become a social worker. But she has no clear fix yet on her future.

Matt is currently my housemate. Even though his ETS is August 2005, he is likely to return to Iraq; he may get stop-lossed for a year—or more. He'd like to go to college, but he's a pragmatist. He knows the 101st Airborne Division (Air Assault) is going back; everyone does. Fort Campbell always gets deployed—it's a rapid-deployable unit. That's the whole point of the 101st. It isn't like he can avoid it.

As for Shane Kelly, he also moved into my house sometime in the summer after I returned to Fort Campbell. We're still seeing each other. When I see him with his parents, I realize he's a better son to them than I have been a daughter to my parents. I watch him with his own daughter and see what a great dad he is. It really moves me to watch him with her. I also think he's really tough and smart and sexy. We never say the word *love* to each other, and I don't know what's going to happen. But we're trying to work things out.

Even after several operations, Shane still has shrapnel in his head. His traumatic brain injury causes him severe headaches and wicked depressions. He has trouble with his memory, and the medications have not helped much. At Campbell no one could provide him the care or treatment he really needed. They threw pills at him, but nothing worked. Everything was fucked up. Finally, in the late fall of 2004, he moved back to Walter Reed so he could receive better medical care. But there are still tons of problems; the bureaucracy he has to negotiate to get therapy programs has been horrible. This is a man who almost made the ultimate sacrifice for his country. Now he has to fight for everything. What is going to happen to Shane? Does the Army expect a man with a traumatic brain injury to advocate on his own behalf for the care and treatment he deserves? There are days he can barely get out of bed in the morning, the pain is so intense. Watching how shabbily the Army treats Shane—not to mention so many other seriously wounded veterans of this war—has been the deepest disillusionment for me.

Lauren will go back with the Rakkasans to Iraq for another year. She knows it. She's been promoted to corporal and now has her own team; they gave her a team as soon as they could so it would have more cohesion by the time they're deployed. She's training them now. In the meantime we've become very close friends—sharing an occasional night out and a weekly Sunday brunch. Not long ago, I met her parents for the first time. Afterward Lauren said: "I wish you were coming back with me. I wish we were going back together."

It's so hard. So difficult. I feel guilt about it. I know the mission is not over. I still have the desire to go back. Finish what we started. But I need to move on. I need my life not to be on hold anymore. So it's a terrible conflict for me. I want to be free to do what I please, go where I please, live where I please. I don't want to have to file a mileage waiver form every time I travel more than 250 miles from base. I want to visit Europe. Go to museums in Washington, D.C., and take the train up to New York City. Not live in Clarksville, Tennessee.

But I'm not kidding myself. I know the Army can call me back. It's not over. I'm not really done. When I signed my contract in the spring of 2000, it was five years active and then three more years IRR. Inactive ready reserve. If I'm not stop-lossed, and I do get out of the Army in April 2005, I must still keep them informed of my whereabouts. They need to be able to reach me. I can still get a letter. Telling me to come back.

This does happen. I know a girl with my military occupational specialty on IRR who got the letter to come back. So it's not over. I'm not completely safe until 2008. I could be in graduate school. I could have a job I love. And the letter could come. Tomorrow. Next week. Next month. Next year.

No, it's not over. Not for a long while yet.

ACKNOWLEDGMENTS

I want to thank the wonderful men and women with whom I served—and all who serve today. In particular, I am indebted to the soldiers I worked most closely with, both in MI and combat arms. I was privileged to work alongside amazing people, who have shown me how incredible people can be, both in complexity and in the simplicity of our most basic nature. All you soldiers are better than anyone gives you credit for . . . I could never name all of those who touched me, but I will not forget.

My year in Iraq was difficult—but it would have been nearly impossible for me if it weren't for all the support I got from people back home. To everyone who wrote me and sent me packages, thank you—I cannot properly express the difference it made to get letters and treats so regularly. My parents came through with unconditional support when I needed it most. The rest of my family and my friends kept me in their lives while I was away. And complete strangers made sure that we knew we were not forgotten. My sincerest gratitude goes to all of you.

I want to thank Michael, for coming to me with the idea of this book and working so hard to keep it as accurate as possible.

I also appreciate all the hard work by the people at Norton to make this happen, and our agent for helping us get it published at all. Despite everyone's best efforts, errors are inevitable, and I take full responsibility for those that remain in the book.

There have been a few people who helped me survive the past few years relatively whole. Stephanie, Amber, Justin . . . you have been there for me and been honest with me without fail. Brian, you push me when I need a goad and support me when I need comfort. Thank you most of all—I cannot imagine having done this without you.